CAREER CHOICES
for Students of
ENGLISH

by
CAREER ASSOCIATES

Walker and Company
NEW YORK

First published in the United States of America in 1985 by the Walker Publishing Company, Inc.

Published simultaneously in Canada by John Wiley & Sons Canada, Limited, Rexdale, Ontario.

Library of Congress Cataloging in Publication Data
Main entry under title:

Career choices for students of English.

Bibliography: p.
 1. United States—Occupations. 2. College graduates—Employment—
United States. 3. Vocational guidance—United States. I. Career Associates.
HF5382.5.U5C2554   1985   331.7'023   83-40441
ISBN 0-8027-0793-9
ISBN 0-8027-7246-3 (pbk.)

Printed in the United States of America

10 9 8 7 6 5 4 3 2 1

Titles In The Series

Acknowledgments

We gratefully acknowledge the help of the many people who spent time talking to our research staff about employment opportunities in their fields. This book would not have been possible without their assistance. Our thanks, too, to Catalyst, which has one of the best career libraries in the country in its New York, NY, offices, and to the National Society for Internships and Experiential Education, Raleigh, NC, which provided information on internship opportunities for a variety of professions. The chapter on legal careers came about only through the excellent efforts of Lynn Stephens Strudler, Assistant Dean of the New York University School of Law Placement Office; special thanks, also, to the staff of researchers and interviewers who took time from their duties as law placement officers to gather the information in this chapter. The following individuals and organizations were particularly generous with their time and evaluations of the information contained in this book:

Marge Dover, National Association of Legal Assistants
Lynne Jones, Postgraduate Center for Mental Health
William Stolgitis, Society for Technical Communication

CAREER ASSOCIATES

CONTENTS

WHAT'S IN THIS BOOK FOR YOU?

Recent college graduates, no matter what their major has been, too often discover that there is a dismaying gap between their knowledge and planning and the reality of an actual career. Possibly even more unfortunate is the existence of potentially satisfying careers that graduates do not even know about. Although advice from campus vocational counselors, family, friends, and fellow students can be extremely helpful, there is no substitute for a structured exploration of the various alternatives open to graduates.

The Career Choices Series was created to provide you with the means to conduct such an exploration. It gives you specific, up-to-date information about the entry-level job opportunities in a variety of industries relevant to your degree and highlights opportunities that might otherwise be overlooked. Through its many special features—such as sections on internships, qualifications, and working conditions—the Career Choices Series can help you find out where your interests and abilities lie in order to point your search for an entry-level job in a productive direction. This book cannot find you a job—only you can provide the hard work, persistence, and ingenuity that that requires—but it can save you valuable time and energy. By helping you to narrow the range of your search to careers that are truly suitable for you, this book can help make hunting for a job an exciting adventure rather than a dreary—and sometimes frightening—chore.

The book's easy-to-use format combines general information about each of the industries covered with the hard facts that job-hunters must have. An overall explanation of each industry is followed by authoritative material on the job outlook for entry-level candidates, the competition for the openings that exist, and the new opportunities that may arise from such factors as expansion and technological development. There is a listing of employers by type and by geographic location and a sampling of leading companies by name—by no means all, but enough to give you a good idea of who the employers are.

The section on how to break into the field is not general how-to-get-a-job advice, but rather zeroes in on ways of getting a foot in the door of a particular industry.

You will find the next section, a description of the major functional areas within each industry, especially valuable in making your initial job choice. For example, communications majors aiming for magazine work can evaluate the editorial end, advertising space sales, circulation, or production. Those interested in accounting are shown the differences between management, government, and public accounting. Which of the various areas described offers you the best chance of an entry-level job? What career paths are likely to follow from that position? Will they help you reach your ultimate career goal? The sooner you have a basis to make the decision, the better prepared you can be.

For every industry treated and for the major functional areas within that industry, you'll learn what your duties—both basic and more challenging—are likely to be, what hours you'll work, what your work environment will be, and what range of salary to expect.* What personal and professional qualifications must you have? How can you move up—and to what? This book tells you.

You'll learn how it is possible to overcome the apparent contradiction of the truism, "To get experience you have to have experience." The kinds of extracurricular activities and work experience—summer and/or part-time—that can help you get and perform a job in your chosen area are listed. Internships are another way to get over that hurdle, and specific information is included for each industry. But you should also know that the directories published by the National Society for Internships and Experiential Education (Second Floor, 124 St. Mary's Street, Raleigh, NC 27605) are highly detailed and very useful. They are: *Directory of Undergraduate Internships, Directory of Washington Internships,* and *Directory of Public Service Internships.*

You'll find a list of the books and periodicals you should read to keep up with the latest trends in an industry you are considering, and the names and addresses of professional associations that can

---

* Salary figures given are the latest available as the book goes to press.

be helpful to you—through student chapters, open meetings, and printed information. Finally, interviews with professionals in each field bring you the experiences of people who are actually working in the kinds of jobs you may be aiming for.

Although your entry-level job neither guarantees nor locks you into a lifelong career path, the more you know about what is open to you, the better chance you'll have for a rewarding work future. The information in these pages will not only give you a realistic basis for a good start, it will help you immeasurably in deciding what to explore further on your own. So good reading, good hunting, good luck, and the best of good beginnings.

ADVERTISING

A RE you someone who spends as much time looking at the ads in a magazine as at the editorial sections? Do you find yourself wondering how effective certain television jingles are? Are you more interested in finding out who won a Clio than who won a Tony or an Oscar? If you answer yes, or if you even know what a Clio is, chances are you're a good candidate for a career in advertising.

Advertising agencies hire people from a wide variety of backgrounds—liberal arts, communications, business, and psychology among them—because jobs requiring different skills exist in the four major departments:

- **Creative**
- **Media**
- **Research**
- **Account Services**

At most agencies, the greatest number of jobs can be found in the creative department, where ads are written (and designed by people with a visual arts background) and the media department, which deals with planning a marketing strategy and buying air time and space in printed media for the agency's ads. As a copywriter, your communications or English degree will matter less than your actual speaking and writing skills. It is important to be an idea person, able to come up with many approaches to describe a product. If you want to go into media, ease with numbers is a must.

Research, which studies consumers' perceptions of products and advertising effectiveness, also hires entry-level people from a variety of disciplines, although a solid statistical background is a real asset. You must be able to read and interpret data, and have a real interest in the products and consumer reactions to them.

Account Services, where people work hand-in-hand with the clients, is reserved for those who have already gained experience in the industry, and it's the most direct link with clients and a path to management positions. The media department is the surest route to the account group, although some researchers end up there as well. Some large agencies rotate promising candidates through the media, research, and traffic departments on the way to account services.

Although there is good money to be made in advertising at big agencies, the advertising industry offers less security than many media professions. When an agency loses a major client, those who worked on that account are often let go. If enough income is lost, additional cuts may be made in areas not directly involved. Because client satisfaction is paramount, everyone who works at an agency—from top management to department heads to assistants—feels the pressure of getting work out when the client requests it. That often means staying late to make sure that the copy or reports or recommendations are the best job possible given the time constraints the client has set.

Technological advances are increasing the advertising industry's efficiency and organization. More and more research and account people are using microcomputers, for example. New areas for advertising, like cable television and videotex (described below) are creating more opportunities to expand an agency's services.

Job Outlook

Job Openings Will Grow: As fast as average

Competition for Jobs: Keen

New Job Opportunities: One of the hottest new advertising outlets is videotex, an interactive system that connects a keyboard terminal in a viewer's home to a central computer that broadcasts printed matter over telephone wires. The first such system (called Viewtron) began service in the Miami area in 1983 and brought subscribers hot-off-the-wire news and teleservices, such as banking, local restaurant menus, and shopping information.

Geographic Job Index

New York, NY, is the home of major ad agencies, the headquarters of the media and many Fortune 1000 firms, each of which also has an advertising department of its own. Chicago, IL, Los Angeles, CA, and Detroit, MI, are the next largest advertising centers. The advertising industry is growing faster than average in Atlanta, GA, Dallas, TX, and Houston, TX.

Who the Employers Are

ADVERTISING AGENCIES in the United States number more than 6000. Nearly all major advertising is created within agencies, where the vast majority of jobs are. Most agencies are small, but about a third are large organizations, some employing more than 1000 people.

IN-HOUSE AGENCIES can be found at large companies. In-house agencies provide anything from specialized functions to the full range of marketing services, some of which exceed what full-service agencies offer. Packaged-goods companies rely on independent agencies for most of their work, with the exception of TV network placement. Although responsibilities and salaries are comparable to those in independent agencies, there is less competition for creative jobs in corporate environments.

Major Employers

ADVERTISING AGENCIES
   BBDO International, Inc., New York, NY
   D'Arcy-MacManus & Masius, Inc., New York, NY
   Doyle Dane Bernbach International, Inc., New York, NY
   Foote, Cone & Belding, Chicago, IL
   J. Walter Thompson Company, New York, NY
   Leo Burnett Company, Inc., Chicago, IL
   McCann-Erickson Worldwide, New York, NY
   Ogilvy & Mather, Inc., New York, NY
   SSC&B, Inc., New York, NY
   Saatchi, Saatchi and Compton, Inc., New York, NY
   Ted Bates Worldwide, Inc., New York, NY
   Young & Rubicam, Inc., New York, NY

How to Break into the Field

Talent, persistence, assertiveness, and enthusiasm are particularly important ingredients in the job campaign of a would-be ad person. If you cannot creatively and imaginatively sell yourself, chances are you won't be good at selling ideas and products to the public— and employers are quick to sense that.

Large agencies are often in contact with the placement directors at a select number of colleges, so it pays to check with that office on your campus. Large companies with their own in-house agencies sometimes recruit on college campuses. But more often than not, it will be up to you to set up interviews on your own. Find out all you can about the agencies at the top of your list (alumni who work there are often good sources of information).

To land a job in the creative department, you need a portfolio of your writing and ideas. It can include your best work on the school paper or radio or TV station. It's less important that your work was published or used commercially than that it shows originality and imagination.

While portfolios aren't necessary for jobs in the other three major departments, sensitivity to and interest in contemporary tastes and trends and some knowledge of the various media are.

CREATIVE

Writing copy requires a feeling for the language that goes beyond the simple communication of information. Rhythm, syntax, and meaning influence the choice of words that will create the right mood and reaction. Copywriters are well paid for their talent, since their command of the language can move millions to purchase a product. In fact, television commercial copywriters earn more money per word than any other kind of writer.

The best way to break into any agency—large or small—is to show that you're a good idea person who is able to come up with clever phrases, catchy slogans, and eye-catching copy. As a junior copywriter, you will be working as a member of a creative team under the supervision of a more experienced copywriter. You may be expected to write copy for a campaign, or you may have to come up with some original ideas for selling a product or service. Depending on the size of the agency and the importance of the campaign, you may be invited to take part in brainstorming sessions, where a group of creative people toss out ideas for a new campaign.

Qualifications

Personal: Good interpersonal skills. A good imagination. Persuasiveness. A strong enough ego to withstand frequent criticism. Sensitivity to current trends. Enormous enthusiasm. Ability to work under pressure.

Professional: Strong language and writing skills. Knowledge of the media.

Career Paths

LEVEL	JOB TITLE	EXPERIENCE NEEDED
Entry	Junior copywriter	College degree
2	Copywriter	1-3 years
3	Senior copywriter	7-10 years
4	Copy chief	10+ years

Job Responsibilities

Entry Level

THE BASICS: Learning about the client or clients from printed material and past correspondence. In small agencies: Answering the phone. Typing. Filing. Drafting simple correspondence.

MORE CHALLENGING DUTIES: Writing descriptive copy. Coming up with concepts for new ad campaigns. Working with the art department on presentations.

Moving Up

Your success will be linked to the success of your creative group at a large agency; at a small one, your effectiveness depends directly on your own contribution. Promotions will be based on your consistently good ideas and great copy. Moving up may mean getting a more significant role to play on a national account or being switched to a more prestigious client. With several years' experience and a solid track record, you may become a supervisor of other copywriters and work with the media and account groups developing ad campaign concepts.

MEDIA

A sound strategy for the placement of ads is the job of media planners, who must reduce quantities of raw numerical material to arrive at the most cost-effective way of reaching potential buyers.

As an assistant, you'll be assigned to work on an account under the supervision of a more experienced planner. In big agencies, as many as 25 to 30 people from the four major groups (account, creative, research, and media) may be involved in the media planning process, although you'll work primarily with the account services people. Developing a media strategy involves studying the target audience, geography (where customers live), seasonality of a product, reach and frequency (the distribution of ads and how often they should run), and creative considerations (such as the tone of the ad).

You'll spend considerable time using computers and VisiCalc programs, which speed up routine computation. You'll be analyzing research about the product and its customers or potential customers and extracting usable data from such numbers as the CPM (cost per thousand), the cost of reaching 1000 people in the target audience, and the GRP (gross rating points), the number of people reached for a certain expenditure.

Coming up with the right media mix is challenging because there are so many options. Although you'll know the budget the client has allocated for advertising, the media group may well recommend a higher or lower figure.

Once the client approves the media plan, buyers execute the decisions. In small agencies, planning and buying are often done by the same people, but in the larger ones the tasks are separate. Buyers are more marketing and sales-oriented, and negotiation is a big part of their job. Regional spot buyers, who buy air time on regional radio and television, usually aspire to be network spot buyers, because these buyers handle the most expensive advertising purchases of all.

Qualifications

Personal: Strong interpersonal skills. Ability to work as a member of a team. Good judgment. Willingness to assume responsibility for decisions.

Professional: Basic math skills. Ability to make oral presentations to groups. Strong writing skills.

Career Paths

LEVEL	JOB TITLE	EXPERIENCE NEEDED
Entry	Assistant media planner	College degree
2	Media planner	3-5 years
3	Associate media director	5-7 years
4	Media director of planning	7-10 years
5	Media manager of planning and buying	10+ years

Job Responsibilities

Entry Level

THE BASICS: Learning to interpret rate cards of various media. Heavy computation. Doing work sheets. Analyzing audience ratings (such as Nielsen ratings). Writing letters and memos.

MORE CHALLENGING DUTIES: Comparing media alternatives. Preparing for and delivering presentations to clients. Talking to sales representatives from various media. Evaluating media buys.

Moving Up

Although you must demonstrate basic competence with numbers, your promotability largely depends on selling your ideas about a particular campaign both to members of the team and, most important, to the client. Being able to handle pressure and crises will also help you land a place on interesting and challenging accounts. The most desirable ones are packagedgoods accounts, because these clients invest a lot of money in advertising and demand quality service. After three years on packaged-goods accounts, you can often move into account services. Those who enjoy media planning stay on to become managers in that department if they demonstrate talent and administrative skills.

RESEARCH

The research department is the center of market analysis, consumer research, product evaluation, and concept testing—all the considerations that go into the formulation of a marketing strategy or an advertising campaign.

As an entry-level person, your main responsibilities will be to gather and organize data for the more experienced people in the department. You may be doing primary research—designing surveys to test a hypothesis about a particular product or the consumers who may buy it. In addition to deciding what kinds of questions should be asked and their format, you also pinpoint who the survey respondents should be and how they should be questioned. Once you've worked out all the details, you'll hand over the task of actually carrying out the survey to an outside "supplier," a market research firm. The supplier will present you with a summary of the research results, often rows and columns of numbers. Research analysts figure out what patterns and trends the numbers signify and how they should affect the marketing and advertising campaign.

Secondary research involves culling information published by the government, the trade, or other groups. You'll write reports summarizing the results, which may be used by the creative, account services, or media people.

Before an advertising campaign is created and implemented, the key issue researchers focus on is the consumer's perception of a particular product. Once the campaign is executed, the important thing to determine is whether the advertising is being correctly perceived by those for whom it is intended.

Qualifications

Personal: Problem-solving mentality. A logical, analytical mind. Ability to work independently, yet contribute to a team effort. Good organizational skills.

Professional: Good writing skills. Ability to work with statistics. Familiarity with data interpretation.

Career Paths

LEVEL	JOB TITLE	EXPERIENCE NEEDED
Entry	Project director	College or graduate degree. One year of market research experience preferred.
2	Research account executive	1-3 years
3	Associate research director	3-8 years
4	Research director	7-10 years
5	Department manager	10+ years

Job Responsibilities

Entry Level

THE BASICS: Plenty of paperwork. Posting numbers from computer printouts. Researching printed literature.

MORE CHALLENGING DUTIES: Drafting reports from research. Getting competitive bids from suppliers. Sitting in on planning sessions. Suggesting new methods of data gathering. Helping design surveys.

Moving Up

Demonstrating that you are a talented interpreter of the information you collect is critical in getting promoted, as is coming up with innovative ways to test product information, advertising strategy, or new markets. The more you are able to contribute to the success of a campaign, the more likely it is your star will rise quickly. If, on top of talents for research and analysis, you prove to be an adroit decision-maker, you can move into a management position. Research can also be a pathway to jobs in the account and media groups for those who are more business-oriented.

ACCOUNT SERVICES

Account executives serve as the link between the agency and the client. They oversee all aspects of an ad campaign, working with all other departments to make sure that problems are solved, that work is completed on time, and that everyone involved knows his or her responsibilities. The creative department looks to the account executive for information about the product and for help in creating campaign ideas. Those in research need direction to determine what information is needed about the product and its potential consumers. The media group works closely with the account executives to develop the best marketing strategy and media mix possible for the amount of money budgeted.

The client relies on the account executive to answer questions, correct misunderstandings, and take care of mistakes. Keeping a client happy can involve hand-holding, pacifying, reassuring, and being available for frequent consultations, while not neglecting other clients or the development of new prospects. Profitability is the bottom-line concern of account executives. Given that financial responsibility, two or more years of experience in the business is usually a prerequisite for a job, although some large agencies train particularly qualified candidates. If you were a business major in college and have worked as an intern or summer employee in product development for a major consumer goods manufacturer or in account services in an advertising agency, you may be considered for such a training program.

Qualifications

Personal: Good judgment. Strong interpersonal skills. Willingness to be on the firing line. Sensitivity to current trends. Leadership qualities.

Professional: Negotiation skills. Advertising or marketing experience. Knowledge of product development and manufacturing. Sales acumen.

Career Paths

LEVEL	JOB TITLE	EXPERIENCE NEEDED
Entry	Account executive trainee	College degree. Advertising-related experience.
2	Account executive	1-3 years
3	Senior account executive	5-8 years
4	Accounts supervisor or manager	10-13 years

Job Responsibilities

Entry Level

THE BASICS: Fielding material from other departments. Taking calls from clients. Keeping in touch with the traffic department on schedules for ads and spots. Monitoring deadlines and pressing creative people for overdue copy. Following through on any marketing needs.

MORE CHALLENGING DUTIES: Meeting with clients. Participating in meetings with other departments. Consulting with the creative department on the ideas for a campaign. Planning an overall strategy for your client. Keeping up-to-date on media rate changes and new media outlets.

Moving Up

Once you demonstrate that you're able to deal effectively with clients and work well with your colleagues in other departments, you'll be given a bigger role on a major account or possibly one or two small accounts of your own. (Even newcomers work on major accounts taking care of all the details for more senior account executives.) It is your responsibility to anticipate and prevent potential problems and confrontations while doing your best for both the agency and the client. Building a successful record of ad campaigns and developing a reputation for being easy to work with can eventually earn you the title of senior account executive.

Only those who are effective managers and have well-honed administrative skills eventually become account managers and supervisors, overseeing and nurturing a number of accounts and going after new business. They hold regular meetings with their sales group to point out prospects and build up a file of potential clients, and they engineer the agency pitch for new business.

ADDITIONAL INFORMATION

Salaries

The trade magazine *Adweek* does an annual salary survey. The following figures, which represent the national median annual salary for each position, are take from the July 1983 issue:

CREATIVE

Copywriter	$25,200
Creative director	$50,000

MEDIA

Media buyer	$16,000
Media planner	$20,000
Media department head	$34,500

RESEARCH

Research services director	$35,000

ACCOUNT SERVICES

Assistant account executive	$19,000
Account executive	$28,000
Account department head	$47,000

Working Conditions

Hours: Deadlines and emergencies are the normal course of business at most agencies. Clients must be satisfied, which often means putting in evening or weekend hours, depending on the pressure your department is under to produce.

Environment: Entry-level people in all departments often work in bullpens, but they generally share an office with one or two others. More experienced people have their own offices—and more privacy. Account people usually rate the most attractive office space because they meet with clients and are responsible for millions of dollars in billing.

Workstyle: Creative, media, and account people spend a lot of time in meetings and presentations—with each other and with clients. When you're not discussing ideas and strategies, you'll be at your desk—working over copy if you're in creative or working with figures if you're in media. Account execs spend a lot of time on the phone with clients. Research staff spend their time designing surveys and working with outside market research firms. The media staff gets a coveted perk—lots of lunches paid for by the media sales representatives.

Travel: Travel opportunities vary according to client needs, your position within the agency, and the size of the account, but, generally speaking, most work is done at the agency.

Extracurricular Activities/Work Experience

Campus newspaper or TV or radio station—writing, editing, space sales

Student-run business (or your own)—promoting, marketing, and selling a product or service

Market research firms—working as an intern or summer employee

Internships

The American Advertising Federation offers a variety of internship possibilities through its members nationwide. The scope of each program and the requirements vary from sponsor to sponsor. A complete list of members, which includes companies with in-house advertising departments and agencies, is available by writing to the American Advertising Federation. Interested students must inquire directly with sponsors, keeping in mind that not all members take interns.

Recommended Reading

BOOKS

Ayer Glossary of Advertising and Related Terms, Ayer Press: 1977

Blood, Brains, and Beer: An Autobiography by David Ogilvy, Atheneum Publishers: 1978

Confessions of an Advertising Man by David Ogilvy, Antheneum Publishers: 1980

How to Put Your Book Together and Get a Job in Advertising by Maxine Paetro, E.P. Dutton: 1980

Madison Avenue Handbook by Peter Glenn Publications, Ltd.: 1983

New Advertising: Twenty-one Successful Campaigns from Avis to Volkswagen by Robert Glatzer, Citadel Press: 1970

Ogilvy on Advertising by David Olgilvy, Crown Publishers: 1979

Roster and Organization of the American Association of Advertising Agencies: 1982-3 (available free from AAAA)

Standard Directory of Advertising Agencies (Agency Red Book), National Register Publishing Company: 1983

PERIODICALS

Advertising Age (weekly), Crain Communications, Inc., 740 North Rush Street, Chicago, IL 60611

Adweek (weekly), Adweek Publications, 820 Second Avenue, New York, NY 10017 (regional editions for East, Southeast, West, Southwest, and Midwest)

Professional Associations

The Advertising Council
825 Third Avenue
New York, NY 10022

Advertising Research Foundation
Information Center
3 East 54th Street
New York, NY 10022

American Advertising Federation
1400 K Street, N.W.
Suite 1000
Washington, DC 20005

American Association of Advertising Agencies
200 Park Avenue
New York, NY 10017

Association of National Advertisers
155 East 44th Street
New York, NY 10017

INTERVIEWS

Susan Montgomery, Age 33
Copywriter
Wells, Rich and Green, Inc., New York, NY

Before I became a copywriter, I worked as a secretary in an ad agency. That's not a prerequisite to a job; it's how I happened to start my career. A friend who worked in the creative department suggested that I could make a lot more money writing copy than typing it. So I went to a school called The Advertising Center in Los Angeles, where I learned advertising concepts, copywriting, and how to put together a portfolio of sample ads. I then went around to various agencies in Los Angeles, but my ad agency friend suggested that if I were really serious about my career, I should go to New York. So I did.

I quickly discovered that when you have a portfolio to show, people are very willing to talk to you. I hardly knew anyone and just began knocking on the doors of various agencies. That's the way to get interviewed. Six weeks after I arrived I was hired by Well, Rich and Green, Inc. If your book is good, sooner or later you'll get a job.

Although I have a degree in English and my education has been useful, my portfolio won me my job. Creative directors are always looking for people who can come up with fresh ideas and solutions to advertising problems. And you have to be able to deal with the people you're working with, who can be difficult at times.

For a person interested in writing, copywriting can be a lucrative way to make a living; however, job security is often out of your control. And losing your job may have nothing to do with you or your work. If the agency loses a big account, a lot of people can be fired because the agency may have supported more people than actually worked on that particular account. That possibility is frightening to some people, but it really doesn't bother me that much.

That's why it's important, throughout your career, to do the best work you can. If that quality is reflected in your portfolio, it won't be long before you're hired.

Al Paul Lefton, Jr., Age 55
President, Chief Executive Officer
Al Paul Lefton Company, Inc., Philadelphia, PA

I started in advertising in 1950 after graduating from Yale. Yale had a divisional major called Sociology, History, and Literature, which I found to be very helpful, especially the sociology courses.

I interview starting-level people. Good grades and the ability to write well and express oneself clearly are essential. The particular academic major is not especially important, but it has to have something to do with words—journalism, English literature, liberal arts.

I would recommend that you do something to make your application different from all the others. I get hundreds of résumés that all look the same. Of course, if the pages are stapled out of order, if postage is due or if the cover letter has misspellings (I get a lot where my name is misspelled!), they go right into the waste-basket.

I am not impressed by gratuitous compliments about our agency that I know are being made about every other agency. I look for applications that show that the writer has done some research, perhaps about a new account we have or that offer some pertinent and interesting observation about a current one.

In the interview, I look for a very high degree of interpersonal skills, fair-mindedness, and balance, for someone who is a good strategist and has a sense of drama and attention to details.

Entry-level positions in advertising often involve a lot of clerical work. The next step on the business side is to an assistant's post, quite often in media or account service. This type of job involves a lot of paperwork and very little decision-making, but it provides the opportunity to learn from firsthand experience. At the next step, account executive, you begin to have some autonomy. It is at this level that you either sink or swim. You have the responsibility for properly servicing an account and making it grow. If you prove to be competent and skillful, you advance to the next level, account supervisor, and beyond that to management supervisor.

Is there security in the agency business? Well, it clearly does not provide the security of a government job. But for all the challenges and diversity of assignments, there have to be risks.

Our industry has gone through remarkable increases in productivity. Twenty years ago, it used to take nine people to handle a million dollars in billings. It now takes only three people per million dollars, and that figure will decline further with increased use of computers, which we now use heavily in testing media schedules and doing in-house typography. Like most fields, advertising has its highs and lows. During those periods when you have to get ready for a sales meeting or put together a presentation which is crucial to the growth of new business, you simply have to postpone your social life. But what I like most about advertising is that you don't do the same thing on any given day. There is always a different kind of client problem to solve.

BANKING

IMAGINE yourself the manager of an operations department, responsible for the global transfer of currencies worth several million dollars. Or a member of the international department, traveling to the Middle East, Africa, or Europe to check on overseas branches. Or managing a loan portfolio for a major multinational corporation, providing its chief financial officer with up-to-date financial information. Banking has become the central nervous system of the world's economy, and today's dynamic banker can be found in front of a desk-top terminal calling up the vast amount of financial data needed to provide an increasing array of new products and services. Today customers want banks to provide more than brokerage services and electronic funds transfers. If you want to be involved in a state-of-the-art business, if you have an entrepreneurial spirit, and, above all, if you are endowed with keen creativity, a career in banking is for you.

The changes in banking are primarily due to the impact of technology. Banking is now a worldwide, 24-hour-a-day business. Automated teller machines, home banking via microcomputers, and office automation have affected every bank employee. But you don't have to be a whiz kid who talks in bits and bytes to get your foot in the door. Every major bank has either a formal training program or professional on-the-job training that includes instruction in the use of the technology. What is most important is your ability to grasp the concept and quickly master the skill.

Banks recruit graduates from a wide variety of majors. In fact, half of all college students entering banking come from a liberal arts background. But don't overlook the traditional financial core courses: business, accounting, marketing, and finance. They will add to your desirability as a job candidate, as will a knowledge of computer science, production management (operations), and interpersonal communications. When a recruiter is having a hard time deciding, it is your interpersonal skills that will count most heavily.

Most banks put their college recruits through a formal training program in which they are taught the methods and practices of the particular institution. Regardless of academic background, all newcomers go into the same melting pot. Students who have taken the financial core courses mentioned will, of course, be more familiar with those subjects during the training program. However, strong analytical skills will enable you to interpret a financial statement, and here an English major who knows how to extract meaning from a careful reading of literature or a history major who knows how to spot a trend or movement in a group of facts will not be at a disadvantage to a finance major.

More and more students entering the field have had the foresight to make themselves knowledgeable about telecommunications to gain an understanding of the newly diverse world of banking. These students have a better chance of getting a job offer than those with a limited, traditional view of the industry.

Many different functional areas exist within banking, and most banks will ask you for which area you prefer to be considered. Commercial and retail banking have recruitment programs in the following functional areas:

- **Credit Lending**
- **Operations**

- **Systems**
- **Trusts**

Job Outlook

Job Openings Will Grow: Faster than average

Competition for Jobs: Keen
Expect the most competition for positions in credit lending. Expanding opportunities can be found in the operations and systems areas. As new sources for loans become harder to find, operations is being looked to for development of nonfee-based services, such as letters of credit and money transfer services. In systems, the computerization and communications systems needed to deliver customer services are implemented.

New Job Opportunities: Because of industry deregulation, banks are now actively seeking people to work in such diverse areas as mergers and acquisitions; private banking, which serves individuals with high net worth and high incomes; office automation, which develops executive information systems and implements them throughout the bank; product management, which includes the planning, pricing, and marketing of new products and services; and telecommunications, which develops the global communications channels necessary for getting and submitting information.

Geographic Job Index

Although banks can be found in any city or town, the major money centers are located in New York, NY, Chicago, IL, San Francisco, CA and Boston, MA. Opportunities at the regional or local end of the industry are growing in Dallas, TX, Houston, TX, and other cities in the Southwest.

Who the Employers Are

COMMERCIAL BANKS (or money-center banks) market their products and services to multinational corporations; to smaller banks, called correspondents; and to individuals, who use checking and loan services.

REGIONAL BANKS provide many of the same services as the larger money-center banks, but on a smaller scale. Their clients are typically locally based small and medium-size businesses.

SAVINGS AND LOAN ASSOCIATIONS offer their customers personal savings accounts and mortgages. However, under new banking legislation, they are allowed to make commercial and business loans.

Major Employers

COMMERCIAL BANKS
> Bank of America, San Francisco, CA
> Bankers Trust Company, New York, NY
> Chase Manhattan Bank, New York, NY
> Chemical Bank, New York, NY
> Citibank, New York, NY
> Continental Illinois National Bank, Chicago, IL
> First National Bank of Boston, Boston, MA
> First National Bank of Chicago, Chicago, IL
> Manufacturers Hanover Trust Company, New York, NY
> Security Pacific National Bank, Los Angeles, CA

REGIONAL BANKS
> First Bank System, Minneapolis, MN
> Mellon Bank, Pittsburgh, PA
> Mercantile Bank, St. Louis, MO
> NCNB National Bank, Charlotte, NC
> Ranier National Bank, Seattle, WA
> Republic Bank Dallas, Dallas, TX
> Wachovia Bank & Trust Company, Winston-Salem, NC

How to Break into the Field

Most banks have formal on-campus recruitment programs through which they hire most of their trainees. They frequently recruit separately for each major functional area: credit lending, operations, systems, and trusts. Be sure to check schedules carefully to ensure an appointment in your area of interest.

Before the interview, do your homework. Learn all you can about the internal workings of the area for which you plan to interview. If your field of interest is not represented, select the next most appropriate area and ask the recruiter to forward your résumé to the proper section. Also, learn something about the bank itself. Different banks have different personalities. Some are aggressive, others more traditional and conservative. Try to interview with banks that have a corporate identity compatible with your own personal identity.

Landing a summer internship is another pathway to a full-time position. Most major banks have internship programs, although they are usually limited to graduate students. Recruitment for the internships is usually done through campus visits. Check with your placement office for details.

If your college does not have a formal placement office, or if the bank to which you wish to apply is not recruiting on your campus, send a well-written letter, accompanied by a résumé, to the bank's director of college recruitment. Follow up your letter with a phone call.

Whether you have an on-campus interview or are writing directly to the college recruitment department, never pass up help from anyone who knows someone at the bank. A well-placed word can be invaluable.

International Job Opportunities

At a large commercial bank, and even at some regional banks, overseas work is possible. International department lending officers may be assigned to work abroad for a period of three to five years, or may be required to travel abroad frequently. Corporate department staffs that handle U.S. multinational corporations also do quite a bit of business overseas.

Most banks try to staff their overseas branches with local citizens. Only the higher-level managerial jobs may be filled by Americans. Specialized positions in areas such as investment banking, joint ventures, and trade go to M.B.A.s or other experienced personnel. Fluency in a foreign language is helpful but not essential, because most banks have contracts with language schools to provide training as necessary.

CREDIT LENDING

This is the most visible area of banking, the area that involves the traditional bank-client relationship that almost everyone associates with the industry. However, this aspect of banking is more than just extending credit or offering interest-bearing accounts to clients. In consumer banking, a lending officer assesses the creditworthiness of individuals. In commercial banking, a lending officer evaluates the financial status of corporations or nonprofit organizations; performs industry surveys, analyzing a particular industry to determine if backing a firm in that area is a good loan risk; makes production forecasts to see if a borrowing firm's available resources will meet production requirements; predicts how a loan would affect the bank's cash flow positively or negatively; or handles corporate overdrafts, contacting corporate customers whose payments are late.

To start out you will go on customer calls with experienced loan officers and be responsible for taking notes and writing a report on the customer and the loan review—not as a participant, but as an observer. You may be called on to research new business prospects, making cold calls to prospects in a given territory or industry. At a smaller bank, your responsibilities will be broader and you will actually make decisions on modest loans quite early.

Qualifications

Personal: Strong analytical skills. Ability to conceptualize. An affinity for quantitative problems. Strong negotiation skills. Extremely good interpersonal skills.

Professional: Ability to analyze data and financial statements and do creative financial planning. Familiarity with bank products and services. Ability to present clearly written reports.

Career Paths

LEVEL	JOB TITLE	EXPERIENCE NEEDED
Entry	Trainee	College degree
2	Assistant Loan Officer	1-2 years
3	Loan Officer/Branch manager	3-5 years
4	Loan manager	7+ years

Job Responsibilities

Entry Level

THE BASICS: Training will consist of both classroom instruction in such areas as finance, accounting, and credit analysis, and actual account work, helping lending officers make judgments about existing or potential bank relationships.

MORE CHALLENGING DUTIES: Upon completion of training, you will be assigned to a line lending area, attend advanced banking seminars, and have the opportunity to meet with customers.

Moving Up

Your advancement will depend on your ability to establish advantageous client relationships, to close lucrative loan deals successfully, and to know when not to approve a loan. As you advance, the loan review process will become more complex and involve significantly more money. You can measure your success by your approval authority—how big a loan you are authorized to approve without going to a higher level of management.

OPERATIONS

The most successful banks anticipate and satisfy all their customers' financial needs. Operations occupies a front-row seat in the banking industry because it has bankwide responsibility for providing customers with nonfee-based (nonloan) services—letters of credit, money transfers, and foreign exchange—services of increased importance because banks can no longer make the profits they once did by lending money to customers. The operations department is usually the largest department of a commercial bank. The Chase Manhattan Bank operations department, for example, has more than 4,000 employees. Graduates are employed in supervisory positions, managing the clerical staff, with responsibility for setting up assignments and time schedules, evaluating performance, making sure work is done properly, training new employees, and authorizing salary increases. Work in operations also involves troubleshooting for customers, solving their account problems, for example, by tracing a money transfer that was never credited.

Qualifications

Personal: Ability to meet deadlines. Ability to perform under pressure. Ability to get along with many different types of people.

Professional: Ability to understand and follow through on complex instructions. Familiarity with concepts of computer science or a related discipline. Knowledge of fee-based services and products.

Career Paths

LEVEL	JOB TITLE	EXPERIENCE NEEDED
Entry	Operations Trainee	College degree
2	Supervisor	18 months
3	Department manager	3-5 years
4	Division manager	6+ years

Job Responsibilities

Entry Level

THE BASICS: You begin your career in operations either in a formal training program, or, more likely, on the job. You will be an operations trainee for about 18 months, learning by rotating among the various departments that handle fee-based services.

MORE CHALLENGING DUTIES: After the training period, you will be assigned to a department or a staff area such as financial management or budget coordination and will learn about a single product or area in depth.

Moving Up

Your progress will depend on your ability to improve the overall productivity of your department or area, to motivate your staff, to stay within your budget, and to complete transactions efficiently, and accurately. Because operations is not exclusively devoted to production management, for further advancement you will need to learn about product development, marketing, and systems functions. Those who move into these areas often accompany loan officers on customer calls, offering the technical advice that will help clinch a deal or presenting a plan to customize an existing product to meet the client's expanding needs.

With hard work and diligence you can acquire the knowledge and expertise that will enable you to move almost anywhere in the bank organization. Operations managers can move into marketing positions, the systems areas, or perhaps relocate (even overseas) to manage a branch bank.

SYSTEMS

The systems area is now involved in every banking decision from credit lending to recruitment. Most large commercial banks have both a central systems area and separate decentralized systems units that service the major components of the organization. Systems is responsible for developing, implementing, and maintaining automated programs for clients and for in-house use; for selecting hardware, writing software, and consulting with the user-client when special programs must be developed. In addition, systems staffers must keep up with the latest developments in technological applications and services.

Qualifications

Personal: Ability to think in analytical terms. Ease in working with abstract models.

Professional: Quantitative skills. Familiarity with the business applications of software and hardware. Ability to convert technical language and concepts into familiar and understandable terms.

Career Paths

LEVEL	JOB TITLE	EXPERIENCE NEEDED
Entry	Systems trainee	College degree
2	Systems analyst	2 years
3	Systems consultant	3 years
4	Senior systems consultant	5 years

Job Responsibilities

Entry Level

THE BASICS: Either in a structured training program or through on-the-job-training, you will become familiar with the bank's hardware and software and how they are used. Depending on your background, you may become a programmer, or you may be placed on a systems team project, refining the use of current equipment or developing systems for as yet unmet needs.

MORE CHALLENGING DUTIES: Applying your skills to more difficult or specialized projects.

Moving Up

If you demonstrate interpersonal skills as well as technical ability, you could become a project manager, overseeing a team of systems people working on the development and implementation of a specific systems capability, such as a new internal telephone switching system or software for an executive work station, which could include features such as electronic mail and word processing.

The potential for a talented systems person is excellent. You could end up managing an operations or office automation department, developing and installing new systems, or becoming a systems consultant for overseas branches. Successful systems personnel can move into any department in the bank.

TRUSTS

The trust department manages and invests money, property, or other assets owned by a client. The pension plans of large corporations and other organizations often use trusts, as do individuals with large assets. Many estates are also managed in trust by the provisions of a will. Like the credit department, this department deals closely and extensively with clients. The training program is similar to that in other areas of banking, but in general advancement is slower and requires more experience.

Qualifications

Personal: A straightforward manner. Accuracy. Good with numbers. Patience in dealing with people. Confidence.

Professional: Strong analytical ability. Good business judgment. Ability to apply financial theory to practical problems.

Career Paths

LEVEL	JOB TITLE	EXPERIENCE NEEDED
Entry	Trainee	College degree
2	Assistant trust officer	1-3 years
3	Trust officer	4-6 years
4	Senior trust officer	10+ years

Job Responsibilities

Entry Level

THE BASICS: Developing familiarity with bank policies and procedures.

MORE CHALLENGING POSITIONS: Researching investments, real estate, or the overall economy to assist superiors. Some contact with clients.

Moving Up

Showing sound judgment and an ability to work independently will garner an assignment to manage some of the smaller trust funds. Moving up also depends on your ability to attract new customers to the bank, as well as to keep present clients satisfied. As you advance you will become responsible for handling more and more money. Top-level trust officers are expected not only to bring in substantial new business and to handle the largest accounts, but also to manage and support lower-level employees.

ADDITIONAL INFORMATION

Salaries

Salaries vary according to the size of the bank. The following figures are taken from Robert Half International's 1984 survey:

Installment loans/assistant manager: $18,000 to $22,000 (small bank); $21,000 to $27,000 (medium-size bank); $23,500 to $28,500 (large bank).

Commercial loans/branch manager: $22,000 to $28,000 (small); $24,000 to $31,000 (medium); $26,000 to $31,000 (large).

Senior loan officer: $28,000 to $32,000 (small); $33,000 to $37,000 (medium); $33,000 to $50,000 (large).

Mortgage loans: $23,500 to $32,000 (small); $28,000 to $36,000 (medium); $32,000 to $41,000 (large).

Operations officer: $17,000 to $21,000 (small); $22,000 to $29,000 (medium); $24,000 to $31,000 (large).

Trust officer: $22,000 to $29,500 (small); $23,000 to $30,000 (medium); $27,500 to $40,000 (large).

Working Conditions

Hours: The credit trainee rarely sees daylight, because long hours and weekend work are often required to get through the training program. After training, normal hours will be whatever it takes to get the job done (nine to five plus). The hours in operations are different because it is a 24-hour-a-day shop. Night shifts and weekend work may be unavoidable, especially for less experienced employees. Systems staffers may also work on a 24-hour clock; the hours are longest when new systems are being installed and deadlines must be met.

Environment: Lending officers get the choicest locations in the bank; because their job is customer-oriented, the surroundings are usually plush and pleasant. The operations and systems departments take a 360-degree turn from the lending department; the workspace is strictly functional, with few amenities.

Workstyle: In credit, much time is spent researching facts and figures about existing and prospective clients, which could take you from the bank library to the client's headquarters. The rest of your time will largely be spent in conference with senior lending officers. Operations and systems work is desk work. Managers walk the area, talking with the staff and lending assistance. In both departments, senior people may meet occasionally with systems consultants.

Travel: Travel is rare for entry-level employees in any bank. Later, however, lending officers in consumer banking might travel throughout their state. In commercial banking, research could take a lending officer to major cities throughout the country. If you are assigned to the international department in credit, operations, or systems, you might be sent to overseas branches.

Extracurricular Activities/Work Experience

Experience as a cashier/teller

Clerical experience

Financial officer/treasurer in campus organizations

Internships

Many banks—savings and loan associations and consumer and commercial banks—are willing to take interns, especially in summer programs. Interns are paid, and the experience may result in a job offer after graduation. Your campus placement office is the best source of information regarding these programs. If your school does not have a placement office, contact the college recruitment director at banks that interest you for details.

Recommended Reading

BOOKS

All You Need to Know About Banks by John Cook and Robert Wood, Bantam Books: 1983

The Bankers by Martin Mayer, Ballantine Books: 1980

In Banks We Trust by Penny Lernoux, Doubleday & Company: 1984

Money: Bank of the Eighties by Dimitris Chorafas, Petrocelli: 1981

Money and Banking by Richard W. Lindholm, Littlefield, Adams & Company: 1969

The New Age of Banking by George Sterne, Profit Ideas: 1981

Polk's World Bank Directory, R. L. Polk and Company (semiannual directory listing banks by city, state, and foreign country)

Your Career in Banking, American Bankers Association: 1980

PERIODICALS

ABA Banking Journal (monthly), 345 Hudson Street, New York, NY 10014

American Banker (daily), One State Street Plaza, New York, NY 10004

The Banker's Magazine (bimonthly), Warren, Gorham, and Lamont, Inc., 210 South Street, Boston, MA 02111

Bank News (monthly), 912 Baltimore Avenue, Kansas City, MO 64105

Professional Associations

American Bankers Association
1120 Connecticut Avenue, N.W.
Washington, DC 20036

Consumer Bankers Association
1725 K Street, N.W.
Washington, DC 20006

National Association of Bank Women
111 East Wacker Drive
Chicago, IL 60601

United States League of Savings Associations
111 East Wacker Drive
Chicago, IL 60601

INTERVIEWS

Louise D'Imperio, Age 22
Operations Analyst
Chase Manhattan Bank, New York, NY

My association with Chase began while I was a student at Villanova University. During summer breaks, I was a member of the apprenticeship management training program, which places undergraduates in operations. The program provides quality relief for full-time employees who take vacations.

I worked in the interbank compensation department, which is responsible for the settlement of funds transfer errors. I worked in the staff support section, which supports the production line. I began by doing simple clerical functions, but later became involved in numbers crunching for production tracking reports. In my final summer, I was an inquiry clerk. My responsibility was to take customer and other bank questions over the phone and via telex and inform the individual of the outcome of the compensation case or reconcile any errors made in settling the case.

In that department I started from the ground up. After three summers, I really knew how a case was initiated and processed, and I had a knowledge of the problems that can arise. But after I graduated in May 1983 I wanted a job outside of bank operations. I have a B.S. in business administration with a concentration in marketing. I wanted a marketing-oriented job and I wanted to be involved in product positioning.

Because I had contacts at Chase, I was able to bypass the normal channels that graduates go through. I looked outside of banking, and mailed résumés to various departments at Chase. Among others, I got a response from Chase international operations and systems.

I chose the position in international operations and systems because I felt that a job in office automation would open up an interesting career path. I knew very little about the field of office automation, but was very interested in it. I work in a division that is concerned with office automation in the international section—more specifically, smaller Chase branches abroad. I'm involved in the marketing and support function of the division, which markets office automation products internally. We want to increase the productivity of individual branches, and we want to increase the use of our products. Our work involves training, consultation, and the development of customized software.

The brunt of my work is project-oriented. Right now I'm working on a project that examines what office automation may do for one of Chase's small subsidiaries. I also edit an office automation newsletter, which takes up about 40 percent of my time, and have written documentation for some of the software developed by our group.

I knew nothing about office automation when I started this job; I actually thought that it involved only word processing. Office automation goes way beyond word processing to include a variety of technologies. My background in operations was not a requirement for this job, but it has made it easier to view the workings of the bank. It also showed me how much I still have to learn about banking. I enjoy my job and I like being involved with technologies that have a definite impact on productivity.

Jayne Geisler, Age 32
Vice President, Market and Financial Planning
Chemical Bank, New York, NY

After receiving a B.A. degree in mathematics and French in 1973 from the State University College of New York at Potsdam, I entered the M.S. teaching program at Boston College, which combined coursework with a part-time teaching position in high school mathematics. Finding teaching unchallenging and realizing my abilities would be better utilized in the business environment, I entered banking, an industry where I felt I could capitalize on my quantitative background

I joined Chemical Bank in 1974 as a financial analyst in the finance, then control, division. My responsiblities included cost accounting and financial management reporting for the consumer banking and upstate regions of the metropolitan (New York) division. Specifically this consisted of preparing, analyzing, and monitoring the financial performance of these business segments against budget and prior years, plus the development of unit and product costs of various banking services. The work was entirely hands-on, with no formal training program, and provided me with a broad understanding of the mechanics of the banking industry.

In 1977 I transferred to the controller's area of the metropolitan division where my duties expanded to include perormance reporting and analysis for the commercial as well as consumer lending areas of the division, acting as a liaison with these areas, plus coordinating their annual budgets. In addition, I was charged with designing and implementing a management information system for evaluating the financial performance of these business segments against budget.

Since 1975 I had been working toward my M.B.A. in finance at night from New York University. Coming from a nonbusiness educational background, I felt that it was apparent that an M.B.A. was necessary to enhance my professional development and my future career goals. It provided me with an understanding of the interrelationships among the key business ingredients—finance, economics, marketing, management, and accounting—which I thought necessary to be more effective in my job. As a result, I am of the opinion that an M.B.A. is an excellent degree for enhancing one's background, especially for those with a liberal arts education. However, I strongly believe that business school is more meaningful and relevant to those who have had prior work experience, as there exists a context in which to augment the course of study.

Upon completion of my M.B.A. in February 1979 I entered the bank's commercial credit training program in order to be a part of the bank's basic business—lending—and to round out my banking experience. I was assigned to the district specializing in the garment/textile/entertainment industries. Handling a portfolio of small business and middle market customers was a challenge. I analyzed and determined credit needs, structured deals, and provided cash management servicing.

Late in 1980 I was asked to join the division's strategic planning unit, which was then undergoing expansion. After a little more than a year as deputy department head, I was promoted to director of the unit, which is my current position. Planning has become increasingly important due to the deregulation of the banking industry. "What do we do now? Where do we want to be in five years? What new products/services should we offer?" These are just some of the challenges facing us as we anticipate the changes in banking law and the movements of our competition. In view of this changing environment created by deregulation, I began working toward a law degree to further supplement my background and experience.

Banking is experiencing tremendous growth and change—it's a whole new ballgame—evolving into a fully integrated financial services industry. The competition not only includes banking institutions, but has expanded to comprise brokerage and investment houses, retailers, high-tech companies, conglomerates, and so forth. As a result, those individuals seeking to enter the industry will need to be sales-oriented and well-rounded in financial services. Banking, finance, and credit will provide the basis, but securities, insurance, and other financial services will play key parts in the banking financial supermarket.

DEPARTMENT STORE RETAILING

CONSUMERS generally take for granted that they will always find their favorite department stores brimming with merchandise. Unnoticed by most customers, a large, talented staff works long, hard hours to keep the shelves filled, the selection varied, the stores beautiful, and the business of retailing running smoothly. Retailing is an industry in which brains and diligence can take you to high levels of decision-making years before your contemporaries in other fields have reached similar positions of responsibility.

Graduates of virtually any discipline may enter department store retailing. Prospective employers are looking for demonstrated capacity to learn and make quick, sound judgments and are less interested in academic backgrounds. You must be flexible, comfortable with people, self-disciplined, and highly motivated—and a sense of humor certainly does not hurt. Retailing is a high-pressure profession where no slow seasons exist—only busy and busier, with the November-December pre-Christmas rush being the most hectic time of all. Prior retail experience, even a summer spent behind a cash register, is a plus; some retailers won't consider candidates without it.

Most entry-level jobs are in merchandising, an area further divided into:

- **Store Management**
- **Buying**

Your job in merchandising begins with a training period of six months to a year. Some trainees divide their time between classroom learning and work experience, others train entirely on the job. Generally, the larger the retailer, the more formalized the training. Whether you enter the field via store management or buying depends primarily on the employer. Many stores separate these functions beginning at the entry level; you must choose which path you prefer. Other stores will introduce all new merchandising personnel to buying and later allow those interested in and qualified for management to move up. The opposite arrangement, moving into buying at some later stage, also occurs, although infrequently.

The modern store is reaping the benefits of the technological revolution. Point-of-sale computer terminals are replacing mechanical cash registers; these automatically compute sales, taxes, and discounts and simplify inventory control by keeping sales records. Computers are also used for credit records and tracking sales forecasts.

Retailing is vulnerable to downturns in the economy, but it's one of the first industries to bounce back after a recession. As a highly profit-oriented business, it's hectic and competitive. The customer's satisfaction and loyalty to the store are very important, which means that you must tolerate and even pamper people whom you may not like. In retailing, the unexpected is the order of the day; you can expect to feel pressured, but seldom unchallenged.

Job Outlook

Job Openings Will Grow: As fast as average

Competition for Jobs: Keen
In merchandising, the most competition exists in buying; this area has fewer openings, tends to pay a bit better, and has an aura of glamour about it.

New Job Opportunities: An exciting new technological development, still in experimental form, that may change retailing in the next decade is video retailing. A select number of communities now have a two-way cable television system through which viewers may receive and send information to a broadcasting center. Viewers can order goods seen on the screen by typing their selections on a keyboard. Video retailing is still in developmental form, but those entering retailing should be aware of its potential as a new job area.

Geographic Job Index

The location of retail jobs parallels the distribution of the general population; stores operate where customers live. As an up-and-coming executive in a retail chain, expect to work in a city or suburban area. Most new store construction in the coming years is expected to take place in revitalizing city cores. Department stores are found across the country, with the highest concentration of jobs in the Northeast, Midwest and West Coast.

If your interest is buying, your geographic options are more limited. For many department store chains, most or all buying takes place in a few key markets, notably New York, NY.

Who the Employers Are

A retailer is, in its simplest definition, a third party who sells a producer's goods to a consumer for a profit. The retailing industry as a whole comprises a wide variety of stores of different sizes with different personnel needs. Management personnel are sought by all major retail firms, including grocery, drug, specialty, and variety store chains, but because the most varied opportunities are found in department stores, this chapter focuses on this sector of retailing.

Major Employers

Allied Stores Corporation, New York, NY
   Bonwit Teller
   Field's
   Jordan Marsh
   Stern's

Carter Hawley Hale Stores, Los Angeles, CA
   Bergdorf Goodman
   The Broadway
   John Wanamaker
   Neiman-Marcus

Dayton Hudson Corporation, Minneapolis, MN
   Dayton's
   Diamond's

Federated Department Stores, New York, NY
   Abraham & Straus
   Bullock's
   Filene's
   Foley's
   I. Magnin
   Rich's

R.H. Macy & Company, New York, NY

Montgomery Ward & Company, Chicago, IL

J. C. Penney Company, New York, NY

Sears, Roebuck & Company, Chicago, IL

How to Break into the Field

Your best bet is on-campus interviews. Major retailers actively recruit on college campuses. This is the most accessible way to most potential employers. Don't hesitate, however, to contact employers directly, especially if you want to work for a smaller operation. Read the business section of your newspaper regularly to find out about store expansions, the addition of new stores or locations, and other developments in retailing that can provide important clues to new job openings. Keep in mind that retail or selling experience of any kind will increase your chances of getting hired.

International Job Opportunities

Extremely limited. Opportunities to live abroad exist at the corporate level of a few international chains.

STORE MANAGEMENT

If you're a "people person," consider the store management side of merchandising. You'll be responsible for handling the needs of staff and customers.

The job of store management personnel, even at entry level, entails making decisions on your own. But since decisions often have to be made on the spot and involve balancing the interests of both customers and the store, your mistakes are likely to be highly visible. Whether you manage the smallest department or a very large store, you must always keep the bottom line—making a profit—in mind when making decisions.

During training, you will work with experienced managers and will be moved throughout the store to observe all aspects of merchandising. If you're quick to learn and demonstrate management potential, you'll soon be made manager of a small department or assistant manager of a large one. You will have a fair amount of autonomy, but you must stick to store standards and implement policies determined by higher level management.

Qualifications

Personal: Ability to learn quickly. Enormous enthusiasm. The flexibility to handle a constantly changing schedule. Willingness to work weekends, holidays, and nights.

Professional: Demonstrated leadership ability. Ability to work with figures, finances, inventories, and quotas. A sense of diplomacy.

Career Paths

LEVEL	JOB TITLE	EXPERIENCE NEEDED
Entry	Department manager trainee	College degree
2	Group department manager	2-3 years
3	Assistant store manager	5-10 years
4	Store manager	8-12 years

Job Responsibilities

Entry Level

THE BASICS: Handling staff scheduling. Dealing with customer complaints. Doing plenty of paperwork.

MORE CHALLENGING DUTIES: Monitoring and motivating your sales staff. Assisting in the selection of merchandise for your department. Making decisions and solving problems.

Moving Up

Advancement in store management depends on how well you shoulder responsibility and take advantage of opportunities to learn. Effectively leading your staff, moving merchandise, and, above all, turning a profit will secure your promotion into higher levels.

Your first management position will be overseeing a small department, handling greater volumes of money and merchandise. The group department manager directs several department managers, coordinating store operations on a larger scale. From here you might progress to assistant store manager and store manager; this last position is, in many respects, similar to running a private business. The best may then go on to the corporate level.

Relocation is often necessary in order to win promotions. Switching store locations every three years or so is not uncommon. However, depending on the chain, a change of workplace need not require a change of address; often stores are within easy driving distance of each other. But the larger the chain, the greater the possibility that you'll have to move to a different city to further your career.

BUYING

Do you fantasize about a shopping spree in the world's fashion capitals? A few lucky buyers, after years of work and experience, are paid to do just that when they're sent to Hong Kong, Paris, or Milan to select new lines of merchandise. Most do not make it to such heights, but on a smaller scale, this is the business of buying.

A buyer decides which goods will be available in a store. Buyers authorize merchandise purchases from wholesalers and set the retail prices. A sensitivity to changing trends, tastes, and styles and an ability to understand and forecast the preference of your own store's customers is crucial. Buyers must also maintain standards of quality while keeping within certain ranges of affordability.

The buyer who works for a discount department store faces a particularly tough job. Obtaining lower-than-average prices for quality merchandise is a real challenge and requires an unerring eye and an ability to negotiate with sellers.

Astute buying translates into profits for the store and advancement for your career. Learning how to spend large sums of money wisely takes practice. Fortunately, as a new buyer you can afford to make a few mistakes, even an occasional expensive one, without jeopardizing your career. A good buyer takes calculated risks, and as you gain experience more of your choices will succeed.

During training, you'll work immediately as an assistant to an experienced buyer. The trainee progresses by observing, asking questions, and offering to take on appropriate responsibilities.

Qualifications

Personal: An interest in changing trends and fashions. An ability to work with a wide variety of personalities. A willingness to channel creativity into a commercial enterprise.

Professional: Financial and negotiating know-how. Organizational skills. Good judgment in spotting trends and evaluating products.

Career Paths

LEVEL	JOB TITLE	EXPERIENCE NEEDED
Entry	Assistant or junior buyer	College degree and store training
2	Buyer (small lines)	2-5 years
3	Buyer (large lines)	4-10 years
4	Corporate merchandise manager	15+ years

Job Responsibilities

Entry Level

THE BASICS: Assisting your supervising buyer. Placing orders and speaking with manufacturers by phone. Supervising the inspection and unpacking of new merchandise and overseeing its distribution.

MORE CHALLENGING DUTIES: Becoming acquainted with various manufacturers' lines. Considering products for purchase. Evaluating your store's needs. Keeping an eye on the competition.

Moving Up

Advancement depends on proof of your ability to judge customer needs and to choose saleable goods. The only purchases closely scrutinized by higher authorities are those inconsistent with past practices and standards.

After completing your training, you will first buy for a small department, then, as you become seasoned, for larger departments. High-placed buyers make decisions in buying for a key department common to several stores, for an entire state, or possibly for many stores. Your buying plans must always be well coordinated with the needs of store management.

ADDITIONAL INFORMATION

Salaries

Entry-level salaries range from $12,000 to $18,000 a year, depending on the employer and the geographic location of the store. Junior buyers tend to be among the best paid entry-level employees.

The following salary ranges show typical annual salaries for experienced retail personnel. In merchandising salaries vary with the size and importance of your department.

2-4 years:	$16,000-24,000
5-10 years:	$22,000-27,000
12 years or more:	$25,000 and up

Working Conditions

Hours: Most retail personnel work a five-day, 40-hour week, but schedules vary with different positions. In store management, daily shifts are rarely nine to five, because stores are open as many as 12 hours a day, seven days a week. Night, weekend, and holiday duty are unavoidable, especially for newcomers. Operations personnel work similar hours. Buyers have more regular schedules and are rarely asked to work evening and weekend hours.

Environment: In merchandising, your time is divided between the office and the sales floor—more often the latter. Office space at the entry level may or may not be private, depending on the store. Whether you share space or not, expect to be close to the sales floor. Merchandising is no place for those who need absolute privacy and quiet in order to be productive.

Workstyle: In store management, office time is 100 percent work; every valuable moment must be used effectively to keep on top of the paperwork. On the floor you will be busy overseeing the arrangement of merchandise, meeting with your sales staff, and listening to customer complaints. Long hours on your feet will test your patience and endurance, but you can never let the weariness show. In buying, office time is spent with paperwork and calls to manufacturers. You might also review catalog copy and illustrations. On the sales floor, you'll meet with store personnel to see how merchandise is displayed and, most important, to see how the customers are responding. Manufacturers' representatives will visit to show their products, and you might spend some days at manufacturer and wholesaler showrooms. Because these jobs bring you into the public eye, you must be well dressed and meticulously groomed. The generous discounts that employees receive as a fringe benefit help defray the cost of maintaining a wardrobe.

Travel: In store management, your responsibility lies with your own department and your own store; travel opportunities are virtually nonexistent, except for some top-level personnel. Buyers, particularly those who live outside major manufacturing centers, may make annual trips to New York, NY, and other key cities. You might also travel to trade shows at which your type of merchandise is displayed.

Extracurricular Activities/Work Experience

Leadership in campus organizations

Treasurer or financial officer of an organization

Sales position on the yearbook or campus newspaper

Summer or part-time work in any aspect of retailing

Internships

Arrange internships with individual stores or chains; many are eager to hire interns, preferring students who are in the fall semester of their senior year. Check with your school's placement or internship office or with the store itself in the spring for a fall internship. Summer internships are also available with some stores. Contact the placement office or the personnel departments of individual stores for details.

Recommended Reading

BOOKS

Buyer's Manual, National Retail Merchants Association: 1979

Creative Selling: A Programmed Approach by R.J. Burley, Addison-Wesley: 1982

The Retail Revolution: Market Transformation, Investment, and Labor in the Modern Department Store by Barry Bluestone et al., Auburn House: 1981

The Woolworths by James Brough, McGraw-Hill: 1982

PERIODICALS

Advertising Age (weekly), Crain Communications, 740 North Rush Street, Chicago, IL 60611

Journal of Retailing (quarterly), New York University, 202 Tisch Building, New York, NY 10003

Stores (monthly), National Retail Merchants Association, 100 West 31st Street, New York, NY 10001

Women's Wear Daily (daily), Fairchild Publications, Inc., 7 East 12th Street, New York, NY 10003

Professional Associations

American Marketing Association
250 South Wacker Drive
Chicago, IL 60606

American Retail Federation
1616 H Street, N.W.
Washington, DC 20006

Association of General Merchandise Chains
1625 I Street, N.W.
Washington, DC 20006

National Retail Merchants Association
100 West 31st Street
New York, NY 10001

INTERVIEWS

Carolyn Egan, Age 33
Fashion Coordinator
Bloomingdale's Department Store, NY

My first job was far removed from retailing—I taught high school math for a year. But the school environment really didn't excite me and I felt I could get more from a job. I saw an ad for the position of fashion coordinator at a branch of Gimbels' department store. I wasn't planning a career in retailing, but because I kept up with fashion and felt I had a flair for it, I applied. I got the job and enjoyed the work, but that particular branch was not a high-caliber store, and after two years I was ready to move on.

I took a part-time job as an assistant manager at an Ann Taylor store, one of a chain selling women's clothing. At that time I was also going to school to finish an art degree. My job included store management and some limited buying. I wound up managing my own store, but because Ann Taylor has a small management staff, I felt there wasn't enough growth potential. I came to know the man who was doing store design for the chain. He was expanding his operations and needed help, so I went to work with him. I designed store interiors and fixtures, which gave me a whole new perspective on the industry. I have been lucky to see so many sides of retailing, but these job changes also required me to relocate.

When I moved into fashion coordination with Bloomingdale's about seven years ago, I finally found what I had been looking for—a high-powered, high-pressured environment. When I walk into the store each morning I feel that things are moving, happening. That's the fun of retailing.

My responsibility is to work with the buyers, helping them choose the right styles. After you've been in retailing a number of years, you know where fashion has been and you can see where it's going. You decide—really by making educated guesses—what the public will want a year from today. My job includes a lot of travel—usually eight or nine weeks a year. Where there are products abroad, we explore them. That's the only way to keep up with the competition.

In buying we speak of hundreds of dozens, so you must be volume-oriented. You ask, "What does our regular customer want to see?" Then you make a decision that has to be more right than wrong. I work with children's wear, a department that rarely sees radical changes in style. But there are always new trends in color and design, and new products.

One of the toughest parts of my job is training new buyers and helping with their first big buys. They are understandably nervous about spending several hundred thousand dollars. The fashion coordinator is one with buying experience. You offer better advice if you understand the pressure and monetary responsibility of the buyer's job.

Even though I'm in a creative area, business and financial concerns are of the highest importance. You must have a head for business in every retailing job. You want to find beautiful quality products, but if they don't sell, you've failed.

The one drawback to my job is advancement. My talents and experience are best used right where I am now. Unlike the buyers, I really have no place higher to go. But I enjoy my work. I suppose it's like being an artist, and how many artists are really appreciated?

G. G. Michelson, Age 58
Senior Vice President for External Affairs
R. H. Macy & Company, NY

My job is a rather unique one—it had never existed before and was tailored just for me. I represent the company in the community in its relationships with government, and in philanthropy. I was the senior vice president for personnel and labor relations in the New York division before moving into the corporate side about five years ago.

I was given this opportunity because of my long association and familiarity with the company and the business. We have a separate public relations department, and I don't interfere with their plans; rather, I am involved in considerations of corporate policy. For example, I handle difficult shareholder and community questions. We have a substantial philanthropy budget to work with. We want to spend this money creatively, but our charitable actions must be in line with our business decisions. We are primarily concerned with the communities in which our stores are located, because we recognize our obligation to those places in which we make our living.

I was quite young when I graduated from college, so I went on to law school to mature and get that valuable credential—but I never intended to practice law. All along I knew that I wanted to work in labor relations.

I considered manufacturing and some of the heavy industries as potential employers, and I came to realize that retailing as a service industry was far more people-intensive than other businesses. I found that in retailing the personnel function had a great deal more status and received more attention from top management. Looking elsewhere, I noticed that the emphasis was on cost control, not people development.

I went directly into Macy's training program from law school. The training program was and, of course, still is largely devoted to merchandising. I worked in merchandising only for the six months that I trained, but that experience gave me an excellent background for understanding the business and the people in it. In employee relations, I had responsibility for hiring, training, and developing our employees and merchandising talent.

In the past ten years, I have seen a significant change in the kind of graduates entering retailing. We now hire a great many graduates who once would have pursued other careers—graduates certified to teach, for instance—and people with liberal arts backgrounds who once would have gone on to grad school. We have always hired people who have broad educations; we have never been too concerned about a candidate's business background. We develop our talent by training people for top management, so we are looking for the ability to learn and grow. We don't want to have to train a person to think for the first time!

I spend a lot of time seeing and counseling young people who are investigating careers. My advice: be expansive and open to unforeseen opportunities. So many graduates have rigid plans—which I jokingly refer to as their "five-year plans." Often the best things that happen in a person's career development are totally unexpected. Bright people should be more flexible than many seem to be.

EDUCATION

M ANY of the world's most prominent citizens have either started their careers as teachers or have added teaching to the list of their accomplishments. Leonardo da Vinci, Leo Tolstoy, Henry Kissinger, and Jimmy Carter are but a few.

Through the ages the theory of education has fascinated many. Tolstoy put off writing his novels in order to work out his ideas about education, and Plato devoted many of his philosophical treatises to exploring how knowledge is transmitted from teacher to student. People teach, he said, not by writing books or making speeches, but by becoming vitally involved in dialogue, in human relationships. Teaching is something that happens between two people; it is communication, knowledge passing from one to another.

Thousands of years later this still holds true. Ask almost any teacher what constitutes good teaching and he or she will tell you: good teaching is caring for the people you teach.   There are less altruistic reasons for becoming a teacher, however, and if you ask a veteran, he or she will probably start with summer vacation—not to mention the three or four weeks of holidays that can accumulate at Christmas, Easter, Thanksgiving, and the scattered celebrations of America's heroes.

Teaching can often serve personal interests, too. For those who love to act, teaching provides the perfect audience. For those who like to be in charge, teaching is one of the few professions where you start off as the boss. For scholars, teaching is a way to delve further into your favorite subjects.

Of course, teaching is not the ideal state. Although the starting salaries can be commensurate with the job market as a whole, salaries for experienced teachers most definitely are not. Crime in the schools has received a lot of national coverage, but what is called crime by the media usually means discipline problems in the school, such as absenteeism, vandalism, and abuse of drugs or alcohol. But prospective teachers must take into account the disciplinary difficulties some of them will encounter.

Perhaps the most troubling problem facing a person interested in a teaching career is the beating teachers' reputations have taken in the last decade. As the quality of education seems to have gone steadily downward, largely because of factors beyond teachers' control, teachers themselves have had to take on more and more responsibilities—not only in the area of teaching, but in the area of genuine care and concern for their students.

Few professions, however, have more social significance than teaching, and none offers the sense of satisfaction that comes from contributing directly and positively to a young person's future. When Wally Schirra, one of the original seven U.S. astronauts, was asked who was the most influential person in his life, he didn't hesitate to say his second-grade teacher.

As computers become standard equipment in more and more classrooms, teacher applicants with computer skills are in a better position to be hired. The educational value of computers, however, depends on how teachers use them. The computer can be used as an automated taskmaster or, more importantly, as an interactive device. Some programs teach sophisticated skills such as thinking and writing even to very small children. Computers can grab and keep a student's attention, stimulate, and motivate him or her to higher levels of achievement. But it is still up to the teacher to provide the crucial interaction that makes learning possible.

Job Outlook

Job Openings Will: Decline

Competition For Jobs: Keen

New Job Opportunities: If current migration trends continue, a 25% decline in the number of 15 to 19-year-olds is projected in the northeast and north central states between 1980 and 1990. The rate of decline is expected to be 15% in the rest of the country. These statistics, combined with the fact that the 61,650 secondary school teacher applicants from the graduating class of 1981 exceeded the number of job openings by 18,150, indicate that new job opportunities are not plentiful. These statistics do not take into account, however, the graduates who applied for and subsequently accepted positions with independent schools.

Because of the recent budget cuts, school systems have suffered severe cutbacks in expenditures in all areas including teacher hiring and salary increases. But positions do exist, especially in math and computer sciences. Many teachers retire, leave the profession, or find administrative positions, creating thousands of openings each year. Willingness to relocate increases their chances of finding a position.

In 1978 a law was passed mandating special education for all handicapped children. The number of special education teachers rose more than 30 percent between 1970 and 1980, to 187,900. The Department of Education is still predicting a shortage of special ed teachers as the population of children needing special education continues to grow. Job supply is not the only incentive for entering this area; generally, special ed teachers are paid anywhere from $500 to $2000 more per year than other teachers.

Many parents are turning to church-affiliated institutions for the education of their children. Although salaries are almost always lower, job prospects in this area will grow.

New opportunities also exist in the areas of continuing education and preschool education. Adult education courses on virtually every subject imaginable are taught all over the country at local libraries and community centers. The need for nursery schools, some operated by teachers from their own homes, is growing as more and more mothers of young children work full- or part-time.

Geographic Job Index

The majority of jobs are found in suburban school systems and city schools; fewer positions are available in rural and remote regions. New York, California, Texas, Pennsylvania, Michigan, and Illinois have the greatest teacher populations and the greatest number of new openings for teachers. Since the southwestern and mountain states are growing considerably in population and school enrollments are on the rise, the need for teachers in those areas is growing at a faster rate than anywhere else in the country.

Who the Employers Are

PUBLIC SCHOOLS
Secondary positions: 925,000
Elementary positions: 1,175,000

PRIVATE SCHOOLS
Secondary positions: 93,000
Elementary positions: 184,000

California leads the country in the number of private schools with 2444. Of these, 1574 are under the auspices of a religious organization. New York, with 1923, comes in second; 1504 of these schools are church-affiliated.

How to Break into the Field

Teacher certification requirements vary according to state and are always handled by the state's department of education. The best way to find out how to be certified in a given state is to seek advice from the education department of your college. Many schools of education are members of the National Council of Accreditation of Teacher Education, and graduates of these schools are most likely to be certifiable in every state. Certain education requirements are necessary for teaching in public schools; for teaching in public or most private high schools, you are also required to have majored in the subject in which you wish to teach. Private elementary and high schools usually do not require either certification or education courses.

College placement offices provide the most information and the best service in the quest for a teaching position. Local school systems keep them informed of openings, and more distant job opportunities can be found on their bulletin boards as well. Information can also be found in the classified sections of local newspapers.

An interesting cover letter and résumé addressed to a principal will usually produce a response or an application form. Visiting the community in which you want to find a job can produce contacts and word of mouth recommendations.

Personal recommendations are always a good way to secure a job, particularly in an independent school. Application to an independent school is made to the headmaster through a letter of introduction, and a résumé that should include any extracurricular activities that would make you a more valuable staff member. The best time to apply is in the fall before the year in which you wish to be employed. Hiring decisions are usually made in March or April.

To save time and gather information about out-of-town schools, it can be useful to contact national placement organizations.

Among these are:

North American Educational Consultants
P.O. Box 995
Barre, VT 05641
802-479-0157
(specializes in secondary schools here and abroad)

Careers in Education
P.O. Box 455
East Stroudsburg, PA 18301

Independent Education Services
80 Nassau Street
Princeton, NJ 08540
800-257-5102 (toll free) or 609-921-6195
(specializes in placing prospective private school
    teachers)

Independent Educational Counselors Association
P.O. Box 125
Forest, MA 02644
(specializes in independent schools for the learning
    disabled)

International Job Opportunities

Opportunities to teach abroad in a variety of subject areas are available to elementary and secondary school teachers through a program sponsored by the United States Information Agency. An applicant must have at least a bachelor's degree, be a United States citizen, and have three years of successful full-time teaching experience, preferably in the subject and at the level for which an application is made. Information and application materials may be obtained from:

Teacher Exchange Branch
United States Information Agency
301 Fourth Street, S.W.
Washington, DC 20547

Opportunities to teach abroad aren't limited to those with three years of teaching experience. For example, speaking Russian can lead you to be sponsored by the American Field Service to partici-pate in an exchange program with the Soviet Union. The Peace Corps, the National Education Association, and UNESCO all offer opportunities for teachers abroad. The most comprehensive brochure on the subject, *Study and Teaching Opportunities Abroad* by Pat Kern McIntyre, can be obtained from the U.S. Department of Education, Washington, DC 20402.

TEACHING

Qualifications

Personal: A genuine desire to work with and care for young people. Ability to lead a group. Strong character. Stamina. Creativity. Well organized.

Professional: College degree. For public schools, certification as well. High school teachers are usually required to have majored in the subject they choose to teach. For elementary school teaching you need a broad range of knowledge and interests, including some instinct for children and how they develop.

Career Paths

LEVEL	JOB TITLE	EXPERIENCE NEEDED
Entry	Teacher	College degree; certification as required
1	Teacher (with master's)	Master's degree in education or in subject area
3	Department Head (high school)	7-10 years

Job Responsibilities

Entry Level

THE BASICS: Presenting subject matter. Developing lesson plans. Preparing and giving examinations. Arranging class and individual projects that contribute to the learning process. Attending parent conferences, field trips, and faculty meetings. In junior and senior high schools, homeroom guidance, study hall supervision.

MORE CHALLENGING DUTIES: Club leadership. Sports coach or leading support for sports activities. Directing activities in which the entire school participates, such as assemblies or fund raisers.

Moving Up

Opportunities for advancement exist in the field of education, especially for those with energy, ideas, and the ability to communicate with both adults and children. Administrators, principals, and superintendents can earn up to $45,000 per year and have a major influence on the communities they serve. To move into administrative or supervisory positions, you must have one year of graduate education, several years of classroom experience, and sometimes a special certificate, depending on the state.

The concept of master teacher is a new one, but school systems in Texas are already awarding teachers who achieve this level—by virtue of experience and effectiveness—with greater responsibility, status and a significant increase in pay. High school teachers have the opportunity to become department heads.

Good and creative teachers with some years of experience are in an excellent position to become educational consultants either as editors of textbooks, directors of special programs, or within the school system as curriculum developers. Especially in the areas of math and the sciences, experienced teachers are being pulled from the classroom to teach other teachers.

To move up in the field of education, you have to have the ability to deal with all kinds of people in all kinds of sensitive situations.

You must have a dedication to the job that continues long after school's over. And you must show a willingness to continue your own education, gaining a master's degree or even a doctoral degree in education or in your subject area.

Teaching can also be a springboard into other professions. Businesses have long known that the experience one gets as a teacher is excellent training for executive positions in marketing, public relations, and advertising. The analytical skills that teachers develop in the classroom, as well as the ability to deal with many different people at many different levels, cannot be taught in a business school. These skills that teachers use day in and day out can be effectively transferred to the business world.

ADDITIONAL INFORMATION

Salaries

Teachers progress in salary as they gain experience. Salaries vary widely from state to state. Starting annual salaries can range from $10,000 to $16,000, but generally higher salaries are to be found in the suburban areas. According to the National Educational Association, for secondary and elementary teachers, in 1982-83, the state with the highest average annual salary was Alaska at $33,953. Washington, DC, came in second with an average salary of $26,045. The lowest paying states were Mississippi, with $14,285; Arkansas, with $15,176; and Vermont, with $15,338.

The salary of an independent secondary school teacher is not commensurate with that of a public school teacher, although there are fringe benefits that can often compensate for the difference in pay. At boarding schools, teachers can expect to receive free room and board or rent-reduced housing on or near campus. Travel expenses and smaller workloads also help to compensate for smaller salaries.

Working Conditions

Hours: Most teachers spend between six and seven hours a day with 15 to 30 children, but that is far from the end of the day. Experienced teachers can often get by with a quick review of their old lesson plans, but new teachers should anticipate an extra two or three hours a day for preparation and correction. Some of the work can be done during the summer vacation and the three or four weeks of holiday during the year.

Environment: This can range from the rolling hills of a rural boarding school to the bleak insides of an inner-city school. Teachers can have access to tennis courts, swimming pools, even a stable full of horses, or they may have to content themselves, for recreation, with the smoke-filled faculty room.

The classroom environment is generally what you make it. Elementary teachers can plaster their walls with children's art, waxed leaves in fall, cutouts of flowers in spring. In secondary schools, decoration can be anything from a chart of chemical elements to a poster of the rock star of the moment.

Workstyle: Most classrooms consist of a blackboard, a big desk, and 20 or 30 smaller ones facing front. Yet each teacher has the choice to make each class either student-centered or teacher-centered. Some teachers prefer to lecture or read to their students; other promote student discussion to various degrees. History teachers have discovered that role-playing and mini-dramas can give life to an epoch. English classes can concentrate on grammar, literature, or writing. With the availability of computers, students are less likely to tune out of math class because of the possibilities for direct interaction and feedback. The art room can offer the freest environment. Many teachers turn on music while students paint or sculpt, and students chat among themselves or with the teacher as they work. The major environmental factor in any class will always be the moods and attitudes of the students, and this is where the good teacher becomes the chief architect of his or her surroundings.

Travel: If travel is your end, teaching abroad can be your means. Class trips and outings are also available to the enterprising teacher. Schools will often pay the expenses of a teacher attending a conference, chaperoning a team to an out-of-town match, or accompanying students to recreational activities.

Extracurricular Activities/Work Experience

Volunteer—Big Brother/Sister program, tutoring, sports, summer camps, teen counseling, child care centers for retarded or culturally disadvantaged children

Athletics—sports (participation can lead to coaching positions in secondary schools)

School—cheerleading, debate society, literary clubs, student newspapers, yearbook publications, student government, drama club, glee club, art club, alumni/admissions administrative work

Internships

Aside from the student teaching that accompanies college or graduate certification and degree programs, there are few opportunities for teaching internships, except at a limited number of independent schools. They offer the opportunity to get experience in teaching without taking on the responsibility of a full-time teacher. Under the tutelage of a head teacher, the intern learns the ins and outs of the profession. Both school and intern benefit from such a program and the intern is often paid a nominal salary. Contact individual independent schools to see if they have a program.

Recommended Reading

BOOKS

Don't Smile Until Christmas: Accounts of the First Year of Teaching, Kevin Ryan, ed. University of Chicago Press: 1970

The Teacher Rebellion by David Selden, Howard University Press: 1970

Teaching School: Points Picked Up by Eric Johnson, Walker & Company: 1979

PERIODICALS

Academic Journal: The Educator's Employment Magazine (biweekly), Box 392, Newton, CT 06470

American Education (ten times a year), U.S. Department of Education, 400 Maryland Avenue, S.W., Washington, DC 20202

Arithmetic Teacher/Mathematics Teacher (ten times a year), 11906 Association Drive, Reston, VA 22091

The Association for School, College and University (ASCUS) Staffing Annual: A Job Search Handbook for Educators (annual), Box 411, Madison, WI 53711

Chronicle of Higher Education (weekly), 1333 New Hampshire Avenue, N.W., Washington, DC 20036

Harvard Educational Review (quarterly), Graduate School of Education, Harvard University, 13 Appian Way, Cambridge, MA 02138

Today's Education (quarterly), National Education Association, 1201 Sixteenth Street, N.W., Washington, DC 20036

Professional Associations

American Federation of Teachers
11 Dupont Circle, N.W.
Washington, DC 20036

Association for School, College and University Staffing
ASCUS Office
Box 411
Madison, WI 53711

National Education Association
1201 Sixteenth Street, N.W.
Washington, DC 20036

INTERVIEWS

Margaret Thompson, Age 39
Secondary School Teacher
Needham High School and Newman Middle School, Needham,
    MA

Although the competition for English teaching positions is very
fierce now, in five or ten years there should be a real market. If
you're lucky enough to find a position right now, though, it can be
the most rewarding experience of your life.

There's autonomy. You're your own boss. Once you're in that
classroom, the door is shut. You can be amazingly creative. Every
single day is a new challenge. And you get to show off a lot.
Probably more than any other subject, teaching English calls on
you to perform.

Teaching English is like conducting an orchestra. You're in
charge, but the students have to play their own instruments. The
more they play their instruments, the happier they are. And when

they can hear those instruments being played together in an orchestra it gives them a big thrill.

For example, sixth and seventh graders are being introduced to literature for the first time in their lives; you teach them about the components of a story—the climax, the development, the resolution; then they read the story and for the first time have a sense of recognition; they're reading about characters who are experiencing some of the same conflicts they are. They listen to each other's interpretations and all of a sudden they don't feel alone anymore.

I think literature is one of the most subtle ways of affecting people's lives. You have to know how to choose the literature that will be the catalyst to self-understanding and give students the structural tools to explore their own lives.

What kind of person would really have fun teaching? A caring person. One who enjoys stroking and being stroked. I've been teaching for 13 years now. I'm making about maximum salary, $26,000 a year. But the feeling of loving more than balances the salary. I'll never stop teaching. It's a joy.

Laura Daigen, Age 29
Fourth-Grade Teacher
New York, NY

I started out teaching Spanish in a high school, but I decided there was a lot more good to be done as a bilingual elementary teacher. I was somewhat disillusioned with the politics of the school where I worked. Teachers who had been there longer made sure that they had no problem students in their classes and that kids with low test scores were taught by the rookies. The Spanish language textbooks were poor and antiquated in their absence of girls and women.

When you're working in a public school in the inner city, the needs of your kids are infinite. There's very little support from the administration or cohesiveness among the faculty. You're alone with kids who have more emotional needs than you can deal with. There is no one to help you help them.

Even under the best of conditions, the hours are long. Sometimes I'm there until six or seven and I'm not the last one to leave. I'm making plans for new curriculum, I'm marking papers, I'm cleaning up the room. You're never finished when you're a teacher: you dream it, you go to sleep thinking about it, and you wake up thinking about it. You're teaching eleven pieces of curriculum and you have to coordinate them and give enough time to each one. It was easier teaching Spanish in a high school, because I was teaching one subject at three different levels and the students had the responsibility of absorbing what you gave them. But when you're teaching elementary school and the kid isn't learning, it's your fault.

If someone were trying to decide whether or not to go into teaching, the first question I would ask him or her is: Do you like kids? Are you ready to take on the responsibility of little human beings and their emotional needs? There is tremendous satisfaction in watching children grow, seeing them move out of themselves and being able to give; recognizing their right to receive fair treatment knowing they can effect change if they see an injustice being done. It feels great to have a kid say, "I like math this year," or "I don't have to try to read these books, I can just read them," or to see kids take charge of their own lives and take pride in what they've done on their own.

I think what makes a good teacher is the sincerity of his or her commitment—whatever it is. It can be to help children love reading or to help them see themselves as important pieces of society or to help them realize the value of their own ethnicity. It has to be more than a vague "I love kids"—but you have to love kids, too.

No matter what I end up doing with my life, I'll always be able to look back on these five or six years and say those were years that I spent doing what I really wanted to do. Perhaps I haven't been well-compensated economically, but the job is rewarding. I will always be able to say that I did something that was meaningful, something that helped others.

LAW

THE practice of law offers a wide variety of career choices for liberal arts graduates. The long arm of the law is an apt phrase not only to describe the law's ability to deal with its violators, but also to point to the fact that the law touches each and every one of us in our daily lives. Few transactions in our complex society—even common ones such as the purchase of a home or a share of stock—are not subject to laws and regulations; skilled interpreters of these laws are in great demand. And everyday lawyer advocates in our nations's civil and criminal courts argue to protect the rights of society and of individuals, and address the fundamental questions of what is fair and just.

The research, writing, and analytical skills of the liberal arts graduate are particularly well-suited to the study and practice of law. Much of a lawyer's work entails reading documents, and then preparing a written presentation of the findings. (For those with a flair for the dramatic, the law also offers the opportunity to argue a case orally in a court.) In its essence this process is one that an English major will find familiar from reading and interpreting poems and novels; the history major will recognize the process from examining and drawing conclusions from historical documents and evidence; the political science major will draw similar parallels from the study of political trends and philosophy.

The majority of lawyers work in one of the following three areas: corporate practice, government service, or private practice. A chapter of this size can only provide the barest outlines of the opportunities available to aspiring lawyers. For this reason an entire book in this series—*Career Choices for Undergraduates Considering Law*—has been devoted to the practice of law.

Job Outlook

Job Openings Will Grow: About as fast as average

Competition for Jobs: Strong to keen

New Job Opportunities: Generally speaking, the outlook for job opportunities with corporations is excellent. Corporations have traditionally depended on private corporate law firms to handle their legal affairs. In recent years, however, many corporations are depending more heavily, and often completely, on inside counsel. The reasons for this trend are largely economic; fees charged by private firms have become so high that most corporations feel they can save money by having their own attorneys on their payroll. Although there will be fluctuations in specific industries caused by economic trends and any other events that would influence business, the general outlook should still remain favorable.

With budget restraints and the current trend toward deregulation and decentralization, there are few growth areas in government service. On the federal side, immigration law is assuming a new importance; on the state and local side, there is a need to take up the slack created by the loosening of federal controls and the decrease in federal services.

Demand for private practitioners rises and falls with national and local shifts in politics and the hot areas in law practice today are mergers and acquisitions, bankruptcy, real estate, and tax, while decreased governmental regulation has lessened the demand for lawyers in such areas as labor law, environmental law, and antitrust. Rapid-fire technological advances—in areas ranging from telecommunications to new life forms—have opened up a new world of job opportunities for lawyers with backgrounds in science and engineering.

Also look for increased job opportunities in areas involving alternatives to litigation as a means of resolving disputes. Current trends include neighborhood justice centers and divorce mediation. The growth in prepaid legal care plans will require increased numbers of specialists to deal with new problems involving such areas as Social Security and worker's compensation.

Geographic Job Index

Work as a lawyer can be found in virtually every city or town in the United States. The most prestigious private firms and largest corporations are naturally located in or near large cities. Work for the federal government is concentrated in Washington, DC, although many U.S. agencies maintain offices in other large population centers. There is a United States Attorney in every state of the union, as well as in Puerto Rico, Guam and the Virgin Islands. State government employment is most often found in the state capital or in the state's largest cities.

Major Employers

CORPORATIONS hire in-house counsel to handle contracts, stock offerings, real estate transactions, labor relations, compliance with government regulations, and any other corporate business for which a lawyer's training is necessary.

GOVERNMENT, state and local—need lawyers to conduct both civil and criminal procedures on their behalf.

firms do not adhere to established timetables. Getting hired is often a matter of making the right contacts and being in the right place at the right time. The hiring criteria are different, too; many of these firms view academic performance as much less important than personality and street smarts.

CORPORATE PRACTICE

Attorneys who work for corporations may wear almost as many hats as their counterparts in private practice. Depending on the size and major business of a corporation, the corporate attorney would be a generalist, coordinating the activities of in-house and outside specialists in many areas of law, or might spend his or her entire career practicing in a highly specialized area of the law.

Areas of specialization for corporate attorneys might include antitrust law, consumer issues, environmental/energy issues, government contracts, government relations, insurance, international law, litigation, personnel/labor relations, product liability, real estate, securities and finance, or tax.

Whether a generalist or a specialist, the corporate attorney does a lot of business planning with the employer. This is different from the practice of a private law firm, where the emphasis is on solving legal problems. The corporate attorney attempts to help the employer plan the affairs of the company so that problems do not arise and the goals of the corporation are achieved in a lawful manner.

Most large corporations do not require specific undergraduate or law school curricula from applicants to their law departments. However, in many cases a business degree or some business background is helpful. Depending on the business of the corporation or the concerns of a specific division in a large law department, a technical undergraduate degree may be required. These would typically include the various areas of engineering and science, and are especially important for an attorney involved in patent law.

Qualifications

Personal: A logical mind. A high moral character. The ability to get along with and work well with others. Tolerance for the sometimes bothersome bureaucratic procedures that are inherent to corporate practice.

Professional: A doctorate of jurisprudence. A license in the state or states in which you will practice. Any additional degrees or training required to follow a particular specialty, such as technical undergraduate degrees for patent law. A firm grasp of the fundamental principles of the law and professional ethics. Excellent research and writing skills.

Career Paths

Although it is impossible to generalize about career paths in corporations, many large law departments do have very structured paths which attorneys are expected to follow. This would usually begin with some sort of training program for one or more years, which gives the attorney an opportunity to become accustomed to the corporation's business procedures and to learn about the various activities of the law department. Work would be done in several areas of law under some supervision. The attorney could then expect to move into a particular area of specialty within the law department and gradually progress to higher levels of responsibility, perhaps including a supervisory position.

In smaller law departments, one might expect a less formal training or introductory period, and greater responsibility from the beginning. There would also be less opportunity to move into a higher position in a smaller corporation. Both small and large corporations sometimes offer attorneys the opportunity to move out of the law department and into other areas, such as planning, sales, or management. In such cases the opportunities often depend on the interests and initiative of the attorney.

PRIVATE LAW FIRMS employ lawyers to deal with individual and corporate clients in every conceivable area of law.

How to Break Into the Field

CORPORATE LAW

All large corporate law departments have organized procedures for recruiting, and most will interview at law schools. Smaller corporations sometimes interview on campus, but will more frequently advertise openings. The smaller the law department, the more likely it is that the employer will prefer attorneys with experience. However, there is a definite trend toward hiring new people directly from law schools. Students should be alert for these opportunities, particularly in businesses experiencing rapid growth. Anyone interested in working for a corporation should not wait for announcements of openings but should do research on possible employers and contact them directly by sending to the head of the law department a résumé and a cover letter that includes the reasons for your interest in the firm.

GOVERNMENT SERVICE

Some federal government departments and agencies interview on campus, although recruiting visits have been cut back in recent years. Other departments, including the Department of Justice, require that an application be submitted. Candidates in whom there is interest are then asked to come in for an interview at regional offices throughout the country. Your law school placement office can supply more detailed information about federal hiring practices, as well as such special programs as the honors program, through which some of the most desirable entry-level positions are filled.

Many of the larger prosecutors' offices conduct interviews on law school campuses in the fall for permanent placement positions beginning the following year. For those students who do not obtain an on-campus interview or who wish to apply to an office that does not have such recruitment efforts, it is best to send a résumé and cover letter to the personnel office, the attorney in charge of hiring, or First Assistant District Attorney. Participation in a criminal law clinic is an especially valuable credential when seeking work in the area.

Some attorney general, city solicitors, and agency offices will interview on law school campuses in the fall for the following year; others may list openings with law schools as they become available. However, many state and city agencies never contact law schools but do hire attorneys at different times throughout the year. The best approach to take is to send a résumé and cover letter directly to each agency or office that interests you and then follow up with a phone call to determine whether any positions exist and the status of your application. It should be remembered that many government civil law offices, both state and local, are controlled by civil service laws. Law students and graduates interested in government careers should be careful to take the civil service exams when they are offered so that they can be ranked on the approved lists.

PRIVATE PRACTICE
There is only one sure formula for getting a job with a large corporate law firm: good grades at a prestigious law school. Large firms typically fill their openings through on-campus interviews, and they strongly prefer to hire students from those schools at which they recruit. If your school does not have a large on-campus recruiting program, a letter-writing campaign to large firms in your geographic area may net you some interviews, but only if you have superb grades or law review experience. Timing is critical, too; large firms do virtually all of their hiring during the August to November recruiting season. It is also important to begin this process during the fall of your second year of law school, because many firms fill most of their permanent openings by making offers to students who have worked for them as summer associates following their second year of law school.

Unlike large firms, which have predictable and recurring hiring needs, small firms usually hire new lawyers only occasionally, and then only when their needs are immediate. Consequently these

Job Responsibilities

Entry Level

In some very large corporate law departments, the beginning attorney's job might resemble an entry job in a large law firm. There will be little or no client contact, and a great deal of research and memo writing, possibly on a very narrow area of the law, or even on one case. However, even in large companies, most corporate jobs involve taking on a great deal of responsibility right away, including client contact as well as whatever research and writing is necessary to handle one's own caseload.

Moving Up

If an attorney stays in the law department, he or she will begin to work on more difficult and important matters, with perhaps more emphasis on business planning. There will also be responsibility for supervising the work of junior lawyers, and for hiring outside counsel when necessary, specifying the work to be done by them and examining all billing to be sure that the corporation has gotten the services it has been asked to pay for.

GOVERNMENT SERVICE

Practicing law for the government can be both a satisfying and a stimulating career choice. Government attorneys are important public servants dedicated to improving the public welfare and preserving the integrity of our judicial system. Government cases often raise challenging legal questions of constitutional dimensions as well as interesting procedural problems. The work requires an attorney who can think analytically, speak and write effectively, and research thoroughly.

With some 5000 lawyers, the U.S. Department of Justice has been described as the largest law office in the world. Its principal function is to represent the United States in court. (The day-to-day lawyering of the federal government—negotiating contracts, providing government officials with legal advice, etc.—is done by lawyers in the office of the general counsel of a department or agency.) There are 93 U.S. Attorneys who function regionally and perform the bulk of the department's litigation; their work is guided by a central staff in Washington, DC. Special case areas such as antitrust, tax, and civil rights are handled by separate divisions within the department. These are based in Washington, DC.

Other federal agencies that employ lawyers include the Securities and Exchange Commission, which monitors and enforces compliance with federal securities laws; the Federal Trade Commission, which is charged with ensuring fair market competition and consumer protection; and the Federal Reserve Board, which is involved with federal regulation of the nation's banking system.

For state and local governments, lawyers can work either in criminal prosecution or in civil law.

Prosecuting attorneys bear an important responsibility in helping to protect society and, at the same time, assuring that accused persons are given fair and impartial treatment within the criminal justice system. Their work is varied and demanding. It requires both an understanding of the procedures governing the trial of criminal matters as well as a knowledge of state or local statutory law and court precedents.

Criminal practice of this nature entails frequent appearances in court, either before a judge or a jury, to argue the legal questions that have arisen and finally to present evidence in the trial of the case. In addition, the work in a district attorney's office involves a range of other important decisions, including determining the validity of arrest procedures, assessing the factual merits of an investigation, and deciding whether to pursue a matter to trial or to bargain for a guilty plea.

State and municipal governments, because of their size and the number of services they provide, need attorneys in almost every specialty area of civil law. Housing, transportation, welfare, mental health, and family services are examples of government services, each of which is governed by its own body of laws.

Attorneys are essential to the provision of these services and to the resolution of a variety of other problems and questions, such as construction contracts, employee disputes, environmental issues, and financial arrangements.

Qualifications

Personal: Dedication to public service. Reliability. Integrity. For criminal prosecutors, the ability to deal with the consequences of criminal brutality. Ability to work well under pressure and with minimal supervision.

Professional: Knowledge of law and procedure, especially as related to the subject area of practice. Excellent writing and communications skills.

Career Paths

Some lawyers remain in government service throughout their careers; others get their early experience with the government and then move on to private or corporate practice; still others move back and forth between government service and other areas of practice.

Lawyers, like all employees who work for the federal government, are assigned a civil service grade. With promotions and continued service your grade (and the pay scale attached to it) rises. In general, promotions within the federal government will net you a wider area of responsibility, more difficult and interesting cases, and supervisory or administrative positions. Lawyers who wish to leave federal employment find that their skills and experience are applicable to private or corporate practice.

There are attorneys who chose to do prosecutorial work for most of their careers and there are others who leave the district attorneys' offices after several years. The litigation experience acquired in a prosecutor's office provides an excellent background for any other litigation or criminal justice position. Many attorneys apply the experience they have gained to the private practice of law.

Those who hold civil law jobs for state or local governments can move into agencies with wider scope, or into supervisory or administrative positions. Those who choose to leave find that their experience is well-respected by the private sector; many attorneys are able to secure positions with law firms and corporations.

Job Responsibilities

Entry Level

THE BASICS: Legal research. Familiarizing yourself with cases and issues. Drafting briefs and memorandums.

MORE CHALLENGING DUTIES: Discussing approaches to a case with other attorneys. Taking depositions. Preparing witnesses. Court appearances. Responding to inquiries from other attorneys, legal employees, or the public.

Moving Up

The competence you display in the performance of your duties is the key to advancement. But winning cases or decisions is not the only thing that counts in the public sector. You must also understand the goals of your agency or division and must work not only toward the successful resolution of your own assignments, but toward the overall achievement of your group.

PRIVATE PRACTICE

The private practice of law offers an exceedingly wide range of career opportunities. No other profession encompasses a greater variety of work experiences than may be found in our country's 168,000 legal establishments—a term that includes small general practice firms, large multi-office firms, and every type and size in between. Such diversity defies generalization, except in the broadest sense; however, private law practice as a whole is clearly a

OTHER AREAS OF PRACTICE

There are three additional major areas of practice that lawyers may choose: politics, public interest law, and teaching.

Jobs in politics include lobbying and legislative positions. An experienced lawyer may choose to run for political office.

Lobbyists are responsible for presenting the positions of the client they represent—which may be a corporation, a trade or professional association, or a public interest advocacy group—to legislative and regulatory bodies, and to government executive departments at federal, state, and even local levels. Successful lobbyists are gregarious and have high energy and enthusiasm. It is a hectic job, sometimes conducted literally in the lobby of a legislative body. A lobbyist must be informed and articulate on the issues in question, and persuasive in presentation—both oral and written—of the client's point of view.

For those with a keen interest in the legislative process, positions on the staffs of legislators and legislative committees are available in Washington, DC, and in the 50 state capitals, as well as with elected officials in the nation's largest cities. The work includes researching and drafting legislation, and dealing with outside lobbyists who may be trying to influence your legislator. If you work for an individual legislator, you may also handle legislative aspects of constituent questions and draft the technical portions of newsletters for the home or state district, as well as advise the legislator on legal issues. Work on a committee is similar, but limited, of course, to the specialized area of the committee's work.

Public interest lawyers represent indigent persons in civil matters, defend indigent persons accused of a crime, or work for one of the many public interest groups that seek to advance their special interests through the legal process.

The Legal Aid Society and the Legal Services Corporation provide lawyers for persons unable to afford counsel to represent them in family and divorce matters, child support claims, probate and other civil matters. Similarly, public defenders—who may be hired by the local government or for whose services local government may contract through a private agency such as the Legal Aid Society—fulfill the obligation of government to provide an attorney for every person charged with a criminal offense, regardless of ability to pay. Lawyers who choose either of these areas of practice must have a willingness to be overworked and underpaid; there are always more cases than lawyers. And the lawyer's need to see justice done must be strong enough to overcome the sheer quantity of human trouble and misery with which he or she must come into contact.

Those who work for public interest groups such as the NAACP, the Sierra Club Legal Defense Fund, and others, spend their time advancing the interests of their group through lobbying, arguing high-impact test litigation, or advising advocates of their group on the legal aspects of their group's aims. Positions with these groups are at a premium, but showing an interest early through volunteer work can help the beginning lawyers find positions that will enable them to work for causes in which they believe.

Teaching is an area that lawyers come to after they have had some experience in private or corporate practice, or with government. As a rule, no special degrees are required beyond the J.D. (Juris Doctor) that is conferred on all law school graduates, although teachers frequently hold an LL.M. (Master of Legal Letters) degree in a specialty area, such as tax or antitrust law. A commitment to the philosophy of the law, to legal education, and to academic research is necessary to make a successful career in teaching. Many teachers, even those with full-time positions, continue to do some outside legal work, either performing services for government or establishing a relationship with a private law firm.

ADDITIONAL INFORMATION

Salaries

Large private practices offer the highest starting salaries for beginning associates—an average of $36,000 per year. Corporations booming business, with gross revenues increasing at a rate of more than 12 percent annually.

Significant among the reasons for this rapid growth rate are the removal of restrictions on attorney advertising; increased numbers of legal clinics and prepaid legal services plans that provide legal services to middle-income groups; and the growing complexity of the economy. These factors have also promoted increased public awareness of individual and collective rights, which in turn provides more work for more attorneys.

Most large law firms are divided into departments along practice lines such as corporate, litigation, real estate, tax, trusts and estates. New associates are usually assigned to one department immediately, but may be given the opportunity in some firms to try out work from a variety of departments before their marriage to a particular area of practice.

Small firms are the backbone of our country's legal system. They provide legal services to small businesses, as well as specialized services for many larger companies. In addition, they handle legal problems for individual clients, including real estate transactions, divorces and other domestic relations issues, estate planning and drafting of wills, personal injury actions, ad defense against criminal charges.

Qualifications

Personal: Objectivity. A high regard for precision and detail. Good organizational abilities. Empathy. Ability to think on your feet and speak well. Physical and mental stamina. Ability to be a team player.

Professional: Excellent legal research and writing skills. Finely honed analytical skills. Counseling and negotiating skills.

Career Paths

In private practice you are either an associate or a partner. An associate is an employee; a partner is a part-owner of the firm. Because of increasing specialization, a few attorneys with in-depth knowledge in a narrow field may be designated permanent associates, but this is only an option in a few very large firms. In large firms, if you are not designated a partner in five to ten years, you are expected to find other employment. At small firms the arrangements are much less hierarchical, and the competition for partnerships is less acute. After several years in private practice attorneys may opt for a corporate spot or for government service, or political or public interest work.

Job Responsibilities

Entry Level

THE BASICS: Legal research and writing. Large firms: rotation through departments, or work on narrow aspects of large cases. Small firms: some client contact from the beginning.

MORE CHALLENGING DUTIES: Large firms: some client contact; responsibility for small cases and projects in their entirety or for more complex aspects of large cases; less structured assignments. Small firms—involvement in all phases of the litigation process.

Moving Up

There is no magic pathway to partnership in a large firm. However, hard work, the ability to get along well with clients and to bring in new ones, and the firm's needs in the associate's area of expertise are all key components. Upward mobility does not cease once an associate becomes a partner, although there are no subsequent title designations to denote prominence. In general, those partners who are responsible for the firm's biggest clients and the most lucrative areas of practice have the strongest voice in firm management and receive the largest shares of the firm's profits.

Opportunities for upward mobility in small firms vary considerably, so it is important for the beginning associate to assess the firm structurally to determine the long-range prospects. Nearly all small firms place great emphasis on a person's ability to bring in new business; in many, a substantial client base is a prerequisite to partnership.

offer the next highest wages, with an average starting wage of $33,000 per year. In government service a beginning lawyer can expect to earn from $20,000 to $25,000 annually. In public interest work and some legislative positions, salaries can be quite low, in the $12,000 to $15,000 per year range.

Working Conditions

Hours: All lawyers work long hours—45 to 50 hours per week is common. Lawyers with large private practice firms, however, often put in much longer hours. In all legal work there will be peak periods—when an important case is being readied for trial, or when a business is negotiating an important contract or merger.

Environment: A lawyer's office can be anything from a handsomely appointed private office in an exclusive building to a battered desk and a chair in a legal clinic in a poor neighborhood. Most lawyers, however, will have surroundings that fall somewhere between these two extremes.

Workstyle: Your workstyle will depend largely on your job. Some lawyers spend most of their time in research and writing, others (such as public defenders) in court, others conferring with clients and other lawyers.

Travel: Travel can vary considerably, but in general it is reserved for more experienced lawyers. A corporate lawyer may be sent to other branches of the company to investigate a series of contracts; lawyers for the federal government may travel to another part of the country to interview witnesses in a case, but a great deal of travel for a beginning lawyer is unusual.

Internships

You will find internships available for nearly every area of law. Many are paying jobs, others offer school credit, still others are volunteer positions. The best place to find out about opportunities is through your law school placement office. If no formal internships exist in the area of your interest, the placement officers may be able to point you in the right direction. Any work experience you are able to garner will help you in your search for full-time employment after graduation. Internships with government agencies and public interest groups tend to be on a volunteer basis. If you must earn money during the summer in order to continue your education, the financial aid office may be able to assist you with finding alternative funding so that you can still get some valuable work experience.

The most formal internship programs exist with large private practice firms. Indeed, students who aspire to large firm practice may find offers of permanent employment difficult to obtain if they have not clerked for a large firm the previous summer. Large firms often go to great lengths to win the favor of top-ranking students.

Judicial Clerkships

Judicial clerkships represent a unique opportunity for new law school graduates to spend an additional year or two learning the law and the judicial process from an expert or scholar—the judge. A clerkship is a mutually beneficial arrangement. The clerk has the opportunity to work one-to-one with and to learn from this scholar, and at the same time to refine basic legal skills. The judge has an eager, bright, articulate new graduate who not only handles the time-consuming jobs of researching points of law and writing the findings into memorandums, but who is able to discuss the issues, act as a sounding board, and play devil's advocate. At its best, a clerkship provides the opportunity to work directly with, study with, and reason with the judge, and to learn the thinking and rationale behind some very difficult decisions. It is an opportunity for a new attorney to get the best possible postgraduate training. Many believe that there is no greater learning experience and no better way to begin a legal career.

Federal clerkships, especially those with higher courts, are the most prestigious, but any clerkship is of immeasurable value. The work sharpens analytic skills and strenghtens writing skills by requiring you to stretch yourself to meet the demands of a sharp and experienced mentor. And it can be an incredible boost to your career. Those who have clerked will be offered plum positions, and the experience puts you into a close working relationship with people who can be important contacts throughout your career.

The competition for clerkships is intense—requiring submission not only of a résumé and school transcript, but of samples of legal writing as well. The final hurdle is the personal interview with the judge, and here chemistry and style will come into play. However, persistence and determination in finding a clerkship can pay off in a greatly enhanced legal career.

Recommended Reading

BOOKS

After Law School? Finding a Job in a Tight Market by Saul Miller, Little Brown & Company: 1978

The American Lawyer Guide to Leading Law Firms, compiled by *The American Lawyer* staff: 1983

From Law Student to Lawyer: A Career Planning Manual by Frances Utley with Gary A. Munneke, American Bar Association: 1984

Good Works: A Guide to Social Change Careers, Karen Aptakin, ed., Center for Study of Responsive Law: 1980

How to Start and Build a Law Practice, 2nd edition. by Jay G. Foonberg, American Bar Association: 1984

I'd Rather Do It Myself—How to Set Up Your Own Law Firm by Stephen Gillers, Law Journal Press: 1980

Lawyering: A Realistic Approach to Legal Practice by James C. Freund, Doubleday & Company: 1982

The Lawyer in Modern Society, 2nd edition. by Vern Countryman, Ten Finman, and Theodore J. Schneyer, Little Brown & Company: 1976

The Lawyers by Martin Mayer, Greenwood Press: 1980

Lions of the Eighties: The Inside Story of the Powerhouse Law Firms by Paul Hoffman, Doubleday & Company: 1982

The Making of a Public Profession by Frances Kahn Zemans and Victor G. Rosenblum, American Bar Foundation: 1981

Martindale-Hubbell Law Directory, Martindale-Hubbell, Inc.: revised annually

Miller's Court by Arthur Miller, Houghton Mifflin Company: 1982

Opportunities in Law Careers by Gary A. Munneke, VGM Career Horizons: 1981

The Partners by James B. Stewart, Simon and Schuster: 1983

Stating Your Case: How to Interview for a Job as a Lawyer by Joseph Ryan, West Publishing Company: 1982

The Washington Want Ads: A Guide to Legal Careers in the Federal Government, Moira K. Griffin, ed., American Bar Association: revised annually

Women in Law by Cynthia Fuchs, Anchor Press/Doubleday: 1983

PERIODICALS

The American Lawyer (monthly), AM-LAW Publishing Corporation, 205 Lexington Avenue, New York, NY 10016.

The National Law Journal (weekly), 111 Eighth Avenue, New York, NY 10011.

Student Lawyer (monthly), American Bar Association, 750 North Lake Shore Drive, Chicago, IL 60611.

Professional Associations

The American Bar Association
1155 East 60th Street
Chicago, IL 60637

National Association of Attorneys General
444 North Capitol Street, N.W.
Suite 403
Washington, DC 20001

National District Attorneys Association
708 Pendleton Street
Alexandria, VA 22134

National Legal Aid and Defenders Association
2100 M Street, N.W.
Suite 1601
Washington, DC 20037

INTERVIEW

Eugune J. Majeski, Age 66
Founding Partner
Ropers, Majeski, Kohn, Bentley, Wagner and Kane, Redwood City, CA

I started the "adventure" as the youngest lawyer in a San Francisco admiralty firm. At that time I knew absolutely nothing about admiralty law—because I had gone to school in Chicago, where there was no great emphasis on admiralty law. But the interesting thing about law is that you don't have to know the specialty in order to become a reasonably good lawyer, because you learn on the job; it's one of the last existing apprenticeship professions.

From the admiralty firm I went to another firm where I began to learn something about litigation, which is, I think, more art than law. I stayed with that firm for three years, generally working for one of the older partners. It was he who decided—30 years ago—to start our firm, and he apparently needed someone to carry his briefcase. I started in that capacity, but when there were only two of us, it was very easy for me quickly to become a "name" partner. We thought we would have a kind of small-town friendly litigation practice, but we are now a large-city litigating firm, because the large city grew around us.

Our firm is involved in all kinds of litigation, except for criminal work. I have principally tried cases in the fields of product liability, malpractice defense, and other civil areas, including actions for libel and slander. About nine out of ten civil cases are now disposed of without trial, though. You see, we have now reached the point where the underlying assumption of many judges is that litigants don't really have to use the court at all because they really should settle everything.

I think that potential lawyers should examine themselves carefully, to be sure that they really want to be a lawyer rather than that they just like the idea of being a lawyer, because the reality is quite different. You put in a lot of hours and you work hard, and you should not be misled into thinking that it's always a joyful, wonderful, exhilarating experience. It is all this, in part, but because the trial is just the tip of the iceberg, and for every day in court you probably spend ten days in preparation, you can see that a lot of the work is drudgery. And it's an even worse situation now, since most cases are now settled out of court.

The satisfaction in litigation is not so much in winning as in doing well in light of your own standards. You may have lost the case, but if you know that you lost it for a lot less than anyone else would have lost it you can be satisfied. Often you know that because of your intervention a more just result occurred. We all recall our great wins, but many other things also give us a feeling of satisfaction.

MAGAZINE AND BOOK PUBLISHING

MAGAZINE and book publishing careers are the goals of many English majors, but it's vital that a graduate have a realistic idea of what the fields involve before choosing either. You should know, for example, that finding the F. Scott Fitzgerald of the eighties is hardly in the cards for any book editor, and that for every coveted staff position on *The New Yorker* or *Time,* there are good, reachable spots on special-interest magazines you may never have heard of, or on trade magazines such as *The Specialty Baker's Voice* or *Railway Track and Structures.*

Just because you have studied literature, do not assume that editorial positions are the only openings suited to your skills. Other departments are not only open to you, but may provide easier entry into the field, and they offer challenging career options. Even though you are not writing and editing, a job in sales or magazine circulation, for instance, still enables you to play a part in the goal of all publishing—to bring the printed word to the public.

For a more detailed discussion of careers in book and magazine publishing, see *Career Choices for Students of Communications and Journalism. Communications and Journalism* also discusses career opportunities in newspaper publishing. Many English majors consider working for a newspaper, but keep in mind that you must have a strong journalism background if you are to compete for an entry-level job in that industry.

Who the Employers Are

Along with the well-known news and consumer magazines, there are many other potential employers.

SPECIAL INTEREST MAGAZINES address the needs of specific groups, such as people interested in a certain sport or hobby.

TRADE MAGAZINES are directed to specific industries and professions.

ASSOCIATION AND ORGANIZATION MAGAZINES often publish magazines that are as slick as those directed to the mass market.

SUNDAY NEWSPAPER SUPPLEMENTS

In book publishing, trade books are the general-interest books, fiction, and nonfiction, sold primarily in bookstores and to libraries. In addition, there are other areas of book publishing.

MASS-MARKET PAPERBACKS are also general-interest books, but are sold in drugstores, supermarkets, and other places where trade books are not found.

EDUCATIONAL AND PROFESSIONAL BOOKS include college, elementary, and high school textbooks; technical and scientific books; and professional handbooks and directories.

RELIGIOUS BOOKS is an area of publishing that involves much more than Bibles and hymnals. Religious publishers bring out titles of interest to both clericals and laypersons. They publish inspirational nonfiction and fiction, and even paperback romances.

How to Break into the Field

If you are resourceful enough to land an internship or summer job at a magazine or book publisher, you'll have an edge over other candidates when you graduate, because you will already have been able to prove your skills. Barring that opportunity, try for personal contacts with someone who can hire you or recommend you for hiring—contacts are important, even for entry-level applicants.

Attending one of the best-known summer publishing institutes provides opportunities to meet such people and expand your knowledge of the industry. For more information, write to the directors:

The New York University Summer Publishing Institute
School of Continuing Education
2 University Place
New York, NY 10003
(magazine and book publishing)

The Radcliffe Publishing Procedures Course
6 Ash Street
Cambridge, MA 02138
(magazine and book publishing)

Rice University Publishing Program (offered alternate
    years)
Office of Continuing Studies
Houston, TX 77001
(magazine and book publishing)

Howard University Press
Book Publishing Institute
2900 Van Ness Street, N.W.
Washington, DC 20008
(book publishing)

University of Denver Publishing Institute
Graduate School of Librarianship
Denver, CO 80208
(book publishing)

In addition, send a well-thought-out and carefully written letter to the editor-in-chief, one of the senior editors, or the head of the department that specially interests you. Work hard on this; unless your letter and résumé are outstanding, they will simply be sent on to the personnel department.

Addresses of publications and publishing houses and names of department heads are listed in the *Literary Market Place* (which concentrates on book publishing, but has information on magazine publishing as well) and the *Magazine Industry Market Place*, both published by R. R. Bowker Company, 205 East 42nd Street, New York, NY 10017.

Employment agencies specializing in publishing placement are worth a try, as are help-wanted ads in newspapers and trade magazines (although with those you'll encounter the most competition).

The typical entry-level position in publishing is the assistant—editorial assistant, publicity assistant, circulation assistant, etc. You are, in a sense, an apprentice, learning the functions of your department by working with experienced professionals. Clerical responsibilities are an inescapable part of any beginning career in publishing. So practice your typing (40 words per minute or more) and realize that performing daily office chores is a prerequisite to advancement.

MAGAZINE PUBLISHING

Editorial

A magazine article, feature, or column may originate with in-house editors or free-lancers. Once an idea is approved, editors and their assistants work with a writer to refine and focus it for their readership and review the finished manuscript for content and style. Editors often cultivate an area of expertise, such as food, travel, fashion, or electronics, and may produce monthly sections or columns on that topic. An editorial job often also requires working with designers, illustrators, or photographers to develop the visual side of an article.

It is possible for an entry-level magazine staffer to progress to writing short articles, but few editors spend much time actually writing. They're more apt to be discussing ideas with writers, polishing copy, turning out blurbs and headlines, and working with the art department on story layout. Senior editors devote their efforts to editing and supervising major stories or whole sections of a publication. Developing article ideas, finding writers to do them, reviewing submissions, and, in general, shaping the issue are the primary editorial responsibilities.

Advertising Sales/Marketing

Ads take up as much as half the page space in a magazine for a very simple reason—ad income provides at least half of the revenue of most magazines. The job of a magazine sales staff is to sell ad space. Magazine salespeople spend much of their time talking to account executives and media planners at ad agencies and at companies whose business they want to cultivate. As a salesperson, you have to convince a potential client that the demographics of your readership match the desired audience. You will pull relevant statistics and information from research done about the particular product or service your potential client wants to promote and use readership studies and surveys prepared by your magazine and by the industry.

The marketing, or sales promotion, department works with sales to develop strategies and provide information that will help the sales staff increase business.

The most successful magazines seldom take on beginners in their sales departments. You must first develop a track record at less well-established publications.

Circulation

This department oversees subscription and newsstand sales. Because advertising rates are based on the average number of copies sold and read, the size of the circulation determines how much money the publication takes in. The key to success is subscriber renewals—dependable readers who will keep buying for years. The high expense of attracting new subscribers can be justified only if circulation has researched and carefully targeted its potential market. Circulation is also responsible for overseeing subscription fulfillment and for collecting overdue bills and canceling unpaid subscriptions.

Career opportunities in circulation vary, depending on the size and setup of the publishing house. The majority of magazine circulation jobs are in subscription, which is always based in-house. Because so few recent graduates consider going into circulation, you stand a good chance of finding a position in this department if you demonstrate a genuine interest in it.

Production

Although magazines are sometimes typeset and always printed outside the company, an in-house staff directs and oversees production work. Besides choosing materials, suppliers, printers, and binders, the production department establishes and enforces schedules for the editorial department. Missed deadlines can increase costs. Production oversees each issue from printer to binder to distributor and subscriber. Complicating this task is the fact that magazines are printed in sections, often at printing plants far removed from one another and the magazine's office. You need a good head for figures and finances and a knowledge of printing materials and the processes of graphic reproduction. Personality and temperament count for a great deal, because you must be able to handle emergencies and resolve last-minute crises before deadline.

BOOK PUBLISHING

Editorial

Book editors have two distinct functions. In the past, these were the dual responsibility of one editor; in smaller houses they still are. But in the larger houses, some editors are acquisition editors, while others do the actual in-house editing.

Acquisition editors bring in books for publication. This involves wining and dining literary agents and established authors, and reviewing manuscripts and proposals that come in "over the transom"—unsolicited—from the authors themselves, after the influx has been culled by an editorial assistant. Another important source of books is the editor's own initiative; a good editor comes up with ideas for saleable books by spotting or seeing an event, a news feature, or a magazine story. The editor then must seek out someone to write the book—possibly an expert in the field, or the author or subject of the published story. Acquiring editors also negotiate book contracts with the author or agent.

In-house editorial responsibilities begin after the manuscript has been acquired. Then the editor works closely with the author, helping with problems, suggesting changes in focus or organization, going over the finished manuscript to improve clarity, accuracy, and appeal. The in-house editor must also see the book through the production process, be involved in the sales and publicity effort, and act as the author's liaison with other departments of the house.

Sales/Marketing/Promotion/Advertising

These four related departments are concerned with getting a book into the marketplace and increasing sales in the stores. A hierarchy of sales personnel sell books to jobbers (wholesalers) and retailers. Top people work in-house; the sales representatives work out of their homes or in satellite offices across the country. Many of the smaller publishing houses do not have their own sales reps, or have only a sales manager and one or two field representatives in selected areas. For their sales, they depend on teams of commission representatives, who sell more than one publisher's line. A job as a commission rep is another entry into the business end of book publishing. For the names and addresses of these organizations, consult the *Literary Market Place*. Sales is the largest of the business-related departments and a source of ample job openings.

The marketing staff, which is smaller, promotes the sale of various book lines, series, or individual titles. (Title is the publishing term for an individual book.) They arrange special sales of books to volume buyers outside traditional book outlets, as premiums, gifts, or special-purpose use. The promotion staff promotes the sales of books in the stores with displays, giveaways, and other devices. They also work to promote the book in the media. Book advertising is limited compared to that of other types of consumer goods, and most is directed to bookstores and libraries. Many books that are not potential best-sellers do well in the marketplace, and some become strong backlist titles, which continue to sell over a long period, and which bookstores must keep in stock. Sales and marketing people must come up with ways to support these books that are neither best-sellers nor duds.

Publicity

The publicity department is responsible for getting authors and their books into the public eye and generating interest in the house's line. A major task is lobbying to get the books reviewed. This department also sends out press releases promoting new books and arranges for author tours and interviews. Author appearances in bookstores, at special events, and at public readings are handled by the publicity department.

Production

The production department is responsible for developing the interior and exterior design of the book, choosing paper, determining production costs, and assuring quality. Once pages have been designed and typefaces chosen, production staffers, working with the designer and editor, will select the paper, the method of printing, and the size of the book.

Production is also responsible for getting the finished books to the wholesalers and retailers. Throughout production, a strict schedule must be followed. The greatest challenge is keeping production costs down while maintaining standards of quality.

In breaking into production, a background in layout, printing techniques, and book design is a plus. You might consider taking one or two book publishing production courses, which several universities offer in their extension curriculum, if your undergraduate major was in a liberal arts subject.

SUBSIDIARY RIGHTS

In large publishing houses, no more than a half dozen people work in this department, yet subsidiary rights is an important income-generating area. The director and staff license the rights to reuse material from the house's books to magazines and newspapers for serialization; to book clubs and paperback houses for reprint; to theaters, movies, and television for dramatization and performance; and to foreign houses for publication abroad. The rights/permissions assistant—the entry position—handles the flow of contracts and correspondence. Rights sales can add prestige to a book, and the significance of their role in a house's income should not be underestimated. Another perk of subsidiary rights can be travel, if you are responsible for foreign sales.

Textbook Publishing

Textbooks make more money per year than books in any other area of publishing, so ample job opportunities exist, primarily for sales reps.

Elementary and high school reps must promote their house's

line with school boards, school administrators, state boards of education, and, at times, individual teachers. School contracts often add up to million-dollar sales and may last for years, so competition is fierce and reps must know their product well and be enthusiastic about it in order to clinch deals. Field reps also play a role in making sure their publishers know about trends in various subject areas so they reflect them in their textbooks.

Sales reps in the college textbook area are known as college travelers. As a traveler, you'll be assigned to visit campuses and meet with professors in a specific geographic area. Besides selling, you may acquire new titles or recruit academics to write or contribute to a new textbook. College travelers often get house and author together.

You'll find the same basic functional areas in textbook houses that exist in trade houses. Experience on the road is a good starting point from which to move into virtually any area. The key to success in all phases of the textbook industry is a clear understanding of the ever-changing educational marketplace, and such experience is only gained through time spent as a field representative.

PARALEGAL PROFESSIONAL

GRADUATES eager to explore a fresh area in which to use the training and traits that have served them as liberal arts majors will welcome this exciting, relatively new career possibility. The inquisitive, analytical mind, concern for detail, and ability to communicate that earned them their degrees are precisely the traits that mark a first-rate paralegal.

The role of the paralegal, also called a legal assistant or sometimes a legal technician, remains to be clearly defined. At the moment, the broadest description of a paralegal is someone who can do everything a lawyer can do, short of arguing a case in court, giving legal advice, accepting clients, setting or accepting legal fees or making legal decisions. In other words, paralegals can do all the varied research necessary for the preparation of any legal proceeding. These duties include drafting legal documents, researching points of law, and investigating the facts of a case; each function involves processing and managing information. Some paralegals deal directly with clients and assist the attorney in court, others do all their work in the office.

The newness of the paralegal profession can be regarded as both the best and the worst thing about it. Because there is no fixed definition of a paralegal's responsibilities, you may be able to carve out your own niche as you demonstrate your abilities. On the other hand, many attorneys, using a paralegal for the first time, may tend to underrate your competence and limit you to basic, unexciting drudge work. The job description is being redefined every time another paralegal and a new employer meet.

The field has grown rapidly as lawyers have begun to recognize how the use of legal assistants improves the efficiency, economy, and availability of legal services. With the paralegal doing the groundwork, the attorney is free to concentrate on developing a strategy for preparing and presenting the case. The role is necessarily a supportive one, and for that reason some people might find the job limiting. But if you are interested in the complexities of the American legal system, but not, for whatever reason, to the extent of pursuing a law degree, paralegal work might be just what you're looking for. It has also proved to be a useful position for those who are thinking about a law career but wish to delay their decision until they know more about what it involves. Many legal assistants have gone on to law school. In some instances, large law firms and corporations have provided aid toward their employees' tuition.

The greatest employment opportunities for paralegals can be found in large law firms. Close behind them are corporations with in-house legal departments, public advocacy groups, and federal and state governments. All these groups will probably employ even more paralegals in the future. The diverse nature of the work done by these employers helps to explain the difficulty in defining the paralegal's job.

In small law firms and public advocacy groups, the role of the paralegal is usually diversified. Because of the limited size and finances of these employers, a paralegal tends to do a little bit of everything. A paralegal working for the government, a large law firm, or a corporate legal department performs more specialized duties. The areas in which paralegals most often specialize include real estate, trusts and estates (inheritance law), litigation, and corporate law. Insurance companies, large banks, and real estate firms have also opened their offices to this new profession.

Sophisticated computer technology, enabling you to process and store information pertinent to a legal case, is rapidly taking over the field. This kind of data processing is known as a computer litigation support system. A single legal case can involve many thousands of documents accumulated over months or even years. The paralegal is responsible for organizing document files, creating indexes, and categorizing data in order to facilitate information retrieval. The data are arranged and cross-referenced according to event, date, subject, individual, and other headings. As computers become increasingly affordable and their use increases, the paralegal becomes increasingly responsible for these litigation support systems. The legal documents for a single case, which once filled several filing cabinets, can now be reduced to a few floppy disks.

Whether you are seated behind your computer console or beside an attorney in a courtroom, you will quickly discover the fascination of law. Weighed against this is the limited opportunity for advancement. A paralegal in a large firm or corporation might be promoted to a managerial position supervising other paralegals. Or a paralegal may become responsible for overseeing larger and more complex cases. Other than that, the only promotions would be in terms of salary and responsibility.

If you are a bright, responsible person who enjoys the challenge of the law, you may have what it takes to be a good paralegal. The experience involving points of law and the use of legal terminology can help you enormously if you later decide to enter law school or to move into another career area.

Job Outlook

Job Openings Will Grow: Faster than average

Competition for Jobs: Keen

New Job Opportunities: At the moment, large law firms are your number one employer and thus offer a better chance for promotion to a managerial position.

Geographic Job Index

Because large firms are the biggest employers of paralegals, the greatest number of jobs will exist in the metropolitan areas where such firms are based. Corporate headquarters, however, are often located outside big cities. Small law firms are scattered all across the country, as are state and local government departments that might hire paralegals. A quick check will tell you if a corporation, law firm, or government agency in your area employs paralegals.

Who the Employers Are

LAW FIRMS with 25 or more lawyers often have a staff of paralegals. The number—from 2 to 30 or more—of legal assistants they employ depends on the firm. In a small law firm, which may consist of 1 or 2 lawyers and rarely more than 15, a single paralegal might serve the entire firm.

CORPORATE LEGAL DEPARTMENTS often have a staff of paralegals who work on such diverse assignments as trademark law, client contracts, stock option plans, employee benefit plans, labor relations, union negotiations, and compliance with government regulations.

GOVERNMENT AGENCIES also employ paralegals. The Departments of Justice, Treasury, and Defense are the largest federal employers of paralegals, although regulatory agencies often use them as well. The duties of paralegals in these positions vary depending on the agency that employs them. State and local governments are hiring more paralegals. Jobs exist in the offices of the district attorney and the attorney general; duties in these local offices are less specialized than in a federal agency and usually concentrate on criminal law.

PUBLIC SERVICE AGENCIES, such as community legal aid associations and consumer advocate agencies that help the poor, the aged, and other persons in need of legal aid, are eager to use paralegals.

These agencies often work under tight budget constraints, and using paralegals helps them keep their costs down. Paralegals in this sector have an opportunity to do a wider variety of tasks and to work more closely with clients. Many do not work directly under an attorney's supervision but instead carry out their duties independently. They sometimes represent clients at administrative hearings. Paralegals who perform such duties are called community service advisers (CSAs) or nonlawyer advocates. Because of large cutbacks in government funding, public service agencies are not doing much hiring at the time of this writing.

How to Break into the Field

Paralegal training is a valuable asset to have when looking for your first job. Courses range from intensive three-month programs to evening and weekend classes at a college or university. Faculties for such programs often include practicing attorneys, and some programs may offer concurrent internships in law offices. The American Bar Association (ABA) publishes a list of paralegal courses that it has approved. You can write to the ABA at: 1155 East 60th Street, Chicago, IL 60637. Training is not always required to land a paralegal position, because many employers feel that the most important training will come on the job. However, more and more law firms are looking for candidates with paralegal training.

Because virtually any law firm may be a potential employer, be prepared to do some exploration. Choose firms and agencies whose work suits your interests, then inquire about their paralegal needs. It is important, particularly in large organizations, to determine who is responsible for hiring paralegals before you apply.

If you would like to work in the federal government, contact a federal job information center or a branch of the Office of Personnel Management and ask for application information. Job openings are often posted at a federal job information center. For jobs with state and local government agencies, contact the appropriate personnel office.

International Job Opportunities

International positions are scarce. There are a few instances of positions with multinational corporations for those fluent in the language and law of a foreign country.

The Work

All legal proceedings depend on facts and information that can be found in documents and legal statutes, or gathered from clients, law libraries, or more technical sources, depending on the case. The organization and management of enormous amounts of information are essential to a case's success. Legal assistants investigate the facts of a case; research the appropriate laws, legal articles, and precedents; and then apprise the lawyer of the information.

Some paralegals interview clients and do trial fact analysis; they even assist at the trial itself. (Public advocates can represent clients at administrative hearings but never at a court trial.) Besides tracking down and processing all the necessary information, a paralegal must keep track of it every step of the way. (Here a computer data base comes into its own.) In addition to pretrial work, paralegals help draft contracts and mortgages.

Qualifications

Personal: Ability to write and speak clearly and concisely, and to extract pertinent facts from a large body of information. Meticulous concern for detail. Extremely well-organized.

Professional: A knowledge of law and legal terminology. Familiarity with computer data base systems is helpful.

Career Paths

LEVEL	JOB TITLE	EXPERIENCE NEEDED
Entry	Paralegal, legal assistant, or legal technician	College degree (and paralegal training)
2	Specialized or experienced paralegal	1-3 years
3	Legal administrator, or paralegal supervisor	3-6 years

Job Responsibilities

Entry Level

THE BASICS: Legal research. Drafting standardized legal documents. Creating legal files.

MORE CHALLENGING DUTIES: Assisting attorney at trial. Interviewing clients. Writing legal recommendations based on your research. Drafting legal documents.

Moving Up

With experience, you will work on more important cases and produce more complex legal research. Promotion varies with the employer. Some paralegals find that to get a better salary and more responsibility they must move to another firm. This is because the paralegal profession is so new. You have to prove to your employer what you are capable of doing and what kind of salary you are worth.

A paralegal who specializes in one area of law can usually command a higher salary. This comes with work experience and on-the-job training, although it can be backed up by a course in the specific area. Large firms and corporations that use specialized paralegals will often pay for an employee's continuing education.

Some paralegals hire themselves out to law firms on a case-by-case basis for hourly pay. Experience is a prerequisite for this kind of free-lance work, but it can be ideal work for those who need a flexible schedule or who prefer to work for themselves. Agencies placing free-lance paralegals are considered a coming trend.

ADDITIONAL INFORMATION

Salaries

A beginning paralegal can expect to earn between $13,000 and $16,000 a year, depending on the size of the employer. With experience your salary may rise to $20,000. The highest paralegal salaries—$20,000 to $25,000—are earned by paralegal supervisors in major corporation and large law firms.

Working Conditions

Hours: Most paralegals work a standard 40-hour-a-week schedule, but hours will vary according to the firm's caseload. If a major case is coming up, or if the firm's caseload is backlogged, you will probably work overtime when the lawyers do.

Environment: The physical space allotted for paralegals varies according to employer. In large law firms with a paralegal staff, it is not uncommon for three or four paralegals to share an office; this is also true in some corporate legal departments and government agencies. In smaller firms, you might be assigned a small office of your own.

Workstyle: Much of your time will be spent at a desk or in a law library. In the more up-to-date firms, you'll find yourself facing a computer terminal most of the day. Some paralegals get out of the office to attend court or to meet clients, witnesses, or representatives of their adversary in a lawsuit.

Travel: Opportunities for travel come up when a case you have researched is tried in another city. Lawyers often take their paralegals to the trial to ensure quick access to necessary information.

Extracurricular Activities/Work Experience

Debating club

Organizing campus events—public speakers, political rallies, class or schoolwide functions. Summer or part-time work for local law firms

Internships

Some students have obtained legal internships while still in college by offering a few hours a week in exchange for experience. Any experience can help you in your quest for your first job. It will also give you a better perspective on the legal profession. If you are interested in public advocacy law, offer your services to a local public service agency. These agencies, always underfunded, seek volunteers, and you would be performing a social service while you learn more about the profession. Local and state government offices offer some internships for college students.

Recommended Reading

BOOKS

Legal Assistants: Update 1981, American Bar Association: 1981

Legal Assistant's Handbook, by Thomas W. Brunner, et. al., Bureau of National Affairs: 1982
The Paralegal: A New Career by Richard Deming, Lodestar Books: 1979

Professional Associations

National Association of Legal Assistants
1420 South Utica
Tulsa, OK 74104

National Federation of Paralegal Associations
P.O. Box 1410
Ben Franklin Station
Washington, DC 20044

INTERVIEW

Patricia Duffy Mordecai, Age 34
Legal Assistant
Heller Ehrman White & McAuliffe, San Francisco, CA

I received my baccalaureate from the University of California at Santa Barbara, where I had majored in political science. I was interested in law and had taken a number of prelaw courses. A career counselor directed me to the legal assistant profession. Even though it was a new profession it seemed interesting and provided the perfect opportunity for me to determine whether I wanted to pursue law school or not.

I found my first job by going through *Martindale & Hubbell,* which is a legal directory. I wrote down the names of all the law firms that were large enough to emply legal assistants and had interesting clients. I sent them letters and enclosed my résumé. On my first job I was assigned to work on a large-scale litigation, which has turned out to be my forte. I've worked now for three firms and, for the most part, on three different cases over a ten-year period.

My second job was with a medium-size law firm that was just beginning to use legal assistants. They had hired a corporate legal assistant and I was to be the first litigation legal assistant. I thought that it would be a real challenge, and indeed it was. Shortly after I joined the firm they got an extremely large case that lasted for the three years that I was there. I went on to oversee that case and during my last year was also promoted to legal assistant coordinator. I feel that I really had an impact on designing the legal assistant program and that I proved to the firm, and a lot of doubtful attorneys, that legal assistants could be used in a positive way. It is always an uphill battle. That's one thing about this profession—you constantly have to prove yourself.

In my present job much of what I do is administrative. I oversee a legal assistant and law clerk staff that exceeds 40 people—all working on one case. I am responsible for overall case management, assist in hiring, and am the main liaison between the 30 attorneys on the case and the legal assistants and law clerks. This position allows me to demonstrate my organizational and managerial strengths.

The trial for the case I am presently managing is still a year away. I am not sure what direction my career will take when the case is over. In a large law firm I have done extremely well; however, there are not many promotions a legal assistant can look forward to. This is a concern I have had throughout my career. If firms want to keep career legal assistants, they must provide sufficient opportunities for them. I enjoy the amount of responsibility I've been given. I like the excitement it generates. It is very satisfying to manage a large team involved in complex litigation.

In large cases, or even medium-size cases, legal assistants are invaluable if they are used correctly. However, if a firm does not provide sufficient incentives for legal assistants to remain, they leave. This often has deleterious effects upon the case, the client, and the firm. All the information and training that person has acquired is lost.

Overall, however, the legal assistant profession has made many advances and continues to provide challenging career opportunities.

TECHNICAL WRITING

Did you ever wonder who wrote those directions for assembling your sound system—the ones that took you hours to decipher? Anyone who has ever purchased a sophisticated piece of electronic equipment has no doubt experienced difficulty following guidelines that are a cinch for technical wizards.

In the past, when manufacturers sold computers and other complex products primarily to technically proficient clients, they didn't need to include anything beyond a manual that listed the equipment's specifications. In the age of the personal computer, however, the quality of technical writing is improving dramatically, primarily because consumers have complained, and have even based buying decisions on the ease with which they can follow the manual that accompanies a product. They want to learn how to operate equipment as quickly and as painlessly as possible, and that means clear and concise support literature.

Although technical writers have long been employed in the automotive, aerospace, precision instrument, and other industries, the computer industry has created an unprecedented need for competent technical writers. And because their work is an important component in the marketing of a company's products, their status, as generalists within a community of scientists, designers, and programmers, has improved dramatically. Because so many of the current job opportunities are in the computer industry, this section discusses those options only.

Technical writers in the computer industry write about two types of products: hardware and software. Hardware is the equipment itself and includes mainframes—the huge computers used by big business—and microcomputers, which are used by individuals in the home and the office. Software refers to the instructions that run computer programs (they're stored on tapes and floppy disks).

A career in technical writing does not require a scientific or engineering background, but it does require an excellent command of the English language and the ability to write logically, clearly, and accurately. Your research and reporting skills must also be sharp, because you must gather all the facts and concepts for your writing from the engineers, systems analysts, and programmers who develop and design the technology. Once you have gleaned the information, your job is to present it to the layperson in an accurate and highly readable manner, so the ability to grasp technical concepts and explain them in easy-to-understand terms is essential.

Technical writers have the luxury of composing and editing their work on state-of-the-art equipment. And although knowing how to use word processing software is a plus, it's not a prerequisite to landing a job. It is helpful, however, to have some experience in layout and design. Technical writers often work with the production staff, which is responsible for the look of the publication. Given the importance consumers place on being able to follow manuals easily, imaginative graphics are critical to the success of support literature.

The technical writing field is small compared to other industries covered in this book, and is growing increasingly competitive. To stand out from the crowd, prospective technical writers must have a strong interest in technology and empathy for the people for whom they'll be writing. Taking one or more computer science or science courses can help you demonstrate your ability to comprehend what you'll be writing about. Although such prior knowledge is desirable, it's not a strict necessity. Having only a limited knowledge of computers may actually sometimes be an asset rather than a liability, because you'll be able to ask the same questions users might have about the product. For many projects you must assume that your audience knows nothing, so if you are able to learn from what you write, it's a good bet your readers will, too. One of the few areas where familiarity with programming would come in handy is if you're expected to write documentation—the technical details written by programmers, and often rewritten by technical writers, that explain how a program was designed.

Job Outlook

Job Openings Will Grow: Faster than average

Competition For Jobs: Some

New Job Opportunities: Microcomputers are the big growth area, and in many instances they are replacing mainframe computers in the business market. While the economic uncertanties faced by many manufacturers of microcomputers may affect the number of new models introduced into the hardware market, the market for software continues to escalate. Integrated software (combining uses of various applications programs) is another trend that will create jobs for technical writers.

Geographic Job Index

Jobs are concentrated in the high-technology centers: California, particularly the area know as Silicon Valley near San Fransico; the Route 128 area of Boston, the North Carolina Research Triangle (Raleigh, Durham, Charlotte area); the Dallas-Fort Worth area of Texas; and the King of Prussia, PA, area near Philadelphia.

Who the Employers Are

HARWARE MAUFACTURERS include companies that are devoted exclusively to the manufacture of computer equipment as well as diversified electronics manufacturers. Many of these companies also write the software that is provided as part of an equipment package to clients and consumers.

SOFTWARE COMPANIES in the United States now number more than 7000, and more are being established all the time. Only the largest among them can afford the luxury of a full-time technical writing staff, but most of them require the assistance of technical writers, if only on a free-lance basis, to help edit and write the literature that accompanies their products. As more and more uses are found for the computer, software companies specializing in new applications will appear. Often called software publishers, these companies produce packaged software programs for micro-computers.

Major Employers

    ADP, Clifton, NJ
    Apple Computer, Cupertino, CA
    Burroughs Corporation, Detroit, MI
    Commodore International, Norristown, PA
    Computer Sciences Corporation, El Segundo, CA
    Computervision Corporation, Bedford, MA
    Cray Research, Minneapolis, MN
    Data General Corporation, Westboro, MA
    DEC, Maynard, MA
    Electronic Data Systems, Dallas, TX
    Hewlett-Packard, Palo Alto, CA
    Honeywell, Inc., Minneapolis, MN
    IBM Corporation, Armonk, NY
    SofTech, Waltham, MA
    Sperry-Univac, New York, NY
    Tandy Corporation, Fort Worth, TX
    Texas Instruments, Dallas, TX
    Wang Laboratories, Inc., Lowell, MA

How to Break into the Field

While high-tech companies don't often come to campuses to recruit technical writers, they do come to recruit computer science and electrical engineering students. If you're resourceful, you might try scheduling an appointment with representatives of companies for which you'd like to work in order to make contact with someone in the company and to find out who does the hiring in your area of interest. If that's not possible, your next best bet is to write directly to the heads of technical writing departments at companies in which you're interested. Responding to help-wanted ads in major Sunday newspapers of the geographic areas listed above and in national trade publications is another route to interviews.

Although plenty of people with communications and even liberal arts backgrounds are being hired as technical writers, an increasing number of employers prefer candidates who have taken some technical writing courses, which are becoming more and more widespread. If your school does not offer technical writing courses, consider taking some at other institutions. Many courses are offered through continuing education divisions of four-year universities. The number of schools developing certificate programs in technical writing is an indication of the growing demand for trained people. Besides familiarizing you with the process of technical writing, such programs are evidence to prospective employers that you have a serious interest in the field. Some programs offer internships as well.

Put together a portfolio of your work, including copy written or edited by you, especially pieces on scientific or technical subjects. Also include examples of technical writing that have not been published but show an employer your abilities.

WRITING AND EDITING

As a technical writer, you will be involved throughout the development of a product. You'll constantly be gathering information from engineers, programmers, and systems analysts so that you can break down a product operation into a series of small steps, find out what to do should the desired result not occur, and anticipate the kinds of problems the uninitiated may have in using the product. This fact-gathering mission can take weeks or even months.

Once you feel you thoroughly grasp how a piece of equipment or program works, you prepare an outline of the material you plan to cover in the instructions. From that you will develop a rough draft. At each stage, it's important to consult with the designers of the product to make sure that you haven't omitted an important fact or step and that the guidelines you've developed incorporate any changes in product design.

As the manuscript is developed and polished, it goes to an editor who checks style, and then back to the technical professionals for a final review for accuracy. People from the marketing and sales staff sometimes review the copy as well. Finally, the material is approved for publication by corporate management. One of the biggest challenges is being accurate in a technical sense while still writing interesting and readable copy—a process that requires many rewrites.

You may be called upon to produce copy that is not directed to the consumer. Engineers and designers sometimes need help preparing speeches or articles for magazines and journals. You might also be asked to prepare important memos or presentations intended purely for in-house use—a confidential new product proposal, for example. Such projects add variety to your work.

Editors represent only a small part of the technical writing staff. Many firms rely on free-lancers or the most experienced technical writers on staff to handle editing needs instead of hiring full-time editors. Ironically, increasingly sophisticated computer software is eliminating many of the functions performed by editors. Programs that correct spelling and basic grammar mistakes are already in use. Programs that analyze sentence construction and spot cliches are also being used on a limited basis. However, the computer will never be able to line edit, that is, to check copy for word usage, organization, and readability, so the need for editors will not entirely disappear. If you prove to be a competent writer, you may be assigned editing responsibilities, which would begin with the routine task of copy editing—checking for spelling and grammar. As you gain more experience, you will begin line editing—questioning content, clarity, and sentence structure—and assume more responsibility for the finished product.

Qualifications

Personal: Patience to work on assignments that may stretch over weeks or months. Flexibility to work on many projects at a time. Strong interpersonal skills.

Professional: Typing. Ability to break down a complicated process into logical steps. Good reporting skills. Ability to write clearly and concisely.

Career Paths

LEVEL	JOB TITLE	EXPERIENCE NEEDED
Entry	Associate	College degree
2	Technical writer	2 years
3	Senior technical writer	5 years
4	Senior editor or department manager	7-10 years

Job Responsibilities

Entry Level

THE BASICS: Proofreading other writers' work. Familiarizing yourself with the style of your company's material. Updating printed copy in need of revision.

MORE CHALLENGING DUTIES: Assisting another writer on a project. Some research and direct contact with technical experts. Learning to work on and use the company's computers.

Moving Up

For the better part of a year, you will be getting informal on-the-job training as you familiarize yourself with company products and publications and work on small projects as the opportunity arises. As you progress, you will do longer, more complicated pieces of technical writing and work on higher-status products. It's essential to keep up with what the competition is doing so that you can incorporate successful techniques into your own work. The more quickly you catch on to the technical jargon used by the professionals around you, the more contact you'll have with technical designers and management. Your progress will depend on your turning in consistently good writing and proving that you can work comfortably with people from academic backgrounds drastically different from your own. Since you're not "one of tem," you may, on occasion, have to tolerate their feelings of superiority because of your lack of technical expertise. Developing tact and diplomacy in dealing with engineers and programmers who may be extremely competent designers but poor writers is also essential.

ADDITIONAL INFORMATION

Salaries

A typical entry-level writer's salary ranges from $18,000 to $20,000 a year. Graduates with proven writing experience and an understanding of technical jargon earn more than those who require more training. Seasoned writers command anywhere from $35,000 to $60,000 a year.

Working Conditions

Hours: Basically nine to five, although overtime often can't be avoided when project deadlines are near.

Environment: The ideal situation, a private office, actually exists for some entry-level people. Others share offices or partitioned work space. A word processor is made available to every writer. The bigger the company, the more comfortable your surroundings will be.

Workstyle: The day is spent largely at your desk, but there are frequent meetings with engineers, editors, marketing personnel, or production staff members.

Travel: Some firms have divisions in different locations, requiring some technical writers to travel, especially when doing research. Extensive or overnight travel is not typically part of a technical writer's job.

Extracurricular Activities/Work Experience

Campus computer center—supervising operation, tutoring, writing instructions for machine use

College newspaper or other campus publications—writing, reporting, editing, proofreading

Society for Collegiate Journalists, Sigma Delta Chi-student member

Recommended Reading

BOOKS

Readings in Technical Writing by David C. Leonard and Peter J. McGuire, Macmillan Publishing Company: 1983

The Soul of a New Machine by Tracy Kidder, Avon Books: 1982

PERIODICALS

Computerworld (weekly), CW Communications, Inc., 375 Cochituate Road, Route 30, Framingham, MA 01701

Infoworld (weekly), Popular Computing, Inc., 530 Lytton Avenue, Palo Alto, CA 94301

Journal of the Society for Technical Communication (quarterly), Society for Technical Communication, 815 Fifteenth Street, N.W. Washington, DC 20005

Professional Association

Society for Technical Communication
815 Fifteenth Street, N.W.
Washington, DC 20005

INTERVIEWS

Betsey Babcock, Age 24
Technical Writer
Data General Corporation, Westboro, MA

My original career plans were very different from what I'm doing now. I was a music major at Wellesley College and planned to enter the field of arts management until I discovered that the salaries were low, there was no job security, and few jobs existed. Going into my senior year, I started to think about alternatives, particularly in the computer field. I had used computers before, but only to play games and do word processing, so I took several programming courses.

I sent out so many résumés to computer companies during my senior year that I suspect I must have contacted every one that ever existed! I was looking for a job in programming; I didn't even know that technical writing existed. Then Data General came to Wellesley to interview for technical writers. I interviewed because I thought I might talk my way into programming, but when I heard about the job, I decided it was tailor-made for me because I like computers and have strong writing skills.

When I started work in July 1981, I was very lucky to be assigned to a new project and to have a boss who wasn't afraid to let me work independently. We were working on an office automation project. I met with the developers, and contributed to the design of the electronic help system that users can call up if problems arise. My first project was to write the "help" messages and tie them to the proper prompts. The software also included an on-line manual, which described the system in detail for those times when the "help" messages weren't enough. It took me a year to write this manual which, when printed out, is two-and-a--half-inches thick!

I've been lucky to get to do design work. It's unusual for a technical writer to do this, but I've developed a reputation for being good at it. The documentation is very much a part of the software, so you have to work hand-in-hand with the developers. Because of my writing, I'm sensitive to the needs of the user, and the designers with whom I work realize that that's a big plus.

I like the creativity required to get a difficult concept across to an unsophisticated audience. You really have to experiment with the right approach and the best organization to use in each project. Working out these details can be exciting.

Although I like writing, I enjoy being involved in design of the products so much that I'm thinking of going into programming— my original goal. As a writer, I sometimes find it frustrating only to be able to suggest revisions in software; programming may give me more influence over the things I want to change.

Bradley Crystal, Age 23
Writer/Editor
Apple Computer, Cupertino, CA

To me, working as a technical writer is an extension of my education. At Stanford University, where I majored in political science, I didn't explore technology as much as I would have liked to. But I've been able to do that at Apple, where I'm surrounded by innovative computer specialists who have tremendous energy and enthusiasm for their work. It's exciting to be here because I really feel that I'm on the cutting edge of technology.

The close ties between Stanford and the nearby Silicon Valley encouraged me to investigate technical writing as a career possibility. My journalism courses and working on the *Stanford Daily* as a reporter, writer, and copy editor prepared me for this job. At the paper we all used video display terminals for writing and editing, so I didn't have to learn that on the job.

Originally, I had applied to work on the *Apple Magazine* (a publication for computer owners that is no longer published), but I was hired to do technical and marketing communications writing. The challenge in my work is to present information in a way that allows the reader to understand the product and to be able to follow the directions. You must be very careful when you write, because you must assume that your readers have a low level of technical know-how.

I've written brochures directed at consumers, but recently I've been working on sales pamphlets, which we supply to dealers and retailers so they can understand our products and explain them to the public. Each is a "pep talk" on why we think our products are viable and saleable.

For a while I copy edited a lot of other writers' work, but I don't do much now. We have a separate copy editing department, but writers are often called on to edit free-lancers' work. Our department has only five writer/editors, and we can't always produce all we are expected to, so free-lancers are often used.

The engineers and designers I work with are usually very helpful. They realize that they operate on a different plane than the public at large. At times they can get bogged down in explaining technicalities and forget that consumers are overwhelmed by too much detail, but it's my job to make sure that doesn't happen. I enjoy being part of the process of educating the public about our products and persuading people that their productivity can be increased through technology.

BIBLIOGRAPHY

The College Graduate's Career Guide by Robert Ginn, Jr., Charles Scribner's Sons: 1981

College Placement Annual by the College Placement Council: revised annually (available in most campus placement offices)

The Complete Job-Search Handbook: All the Skills You Need to Get Any Job and Have a Good Time Doing It by Howard Figler, Holt, Rinehart & Winston: 1981

Consider Your Option: Business Opportunities for Liberal Arts Graduates by Christine A. Gould, Association of American Colleges: 1983 (free)

Go Hire Yourself an Employer by Richard K. Irish, Doubleday & Company: 1977

The Hidden Job Market for the 80's by Tom Jackson and Davidyne Mayleas, Times Books: 1981

Jobs for English Majors and Other Smart People by John L. Munschauer, Peterson's Guides: 1982

Job Hunting with Employment Agencies by Eve Gowdey, Barron's Educational Series: 1978

Making It Big in the City by Peggy J. Schmidt, Coward-McCann: 1983

Making It on Your First Job by Peggy J. Schmidt, Avon Books: 1981

National Directory of Addresses and Telephone Numbers, Concord Reference Books: revised annually

The National Job-Finding Guide by Heinz Uhrich and J. Robert Connor, Doubleday & Company: 1981

The Perfect Résumé by Tom Jackson, Doubleday & Company: 1981

Put Your Degree to Work: A Career Planning and Job Hunting Guide for the New Professional by Marcia R. Fox, W.W. Norton: 1979

The Student Entrepreneur's Guide by Brett M. Kingston, Ten Speed Press: 1980

What Color Is Your Parachute? A Practical Manual for Job Hunters and Career Changers by Richard N. Bolles, Ten Speed Press: 1983

Where Are the Jobs? by John D. Erdlen and Donald H. Sweet, Harcourt Brace Jovanovich: 1982

INDEX

NOTES

NOTES

NOTES

NOTES

NOTES

NOTES

NOTES

NOTES

NOTES

NOTES

NOTES

NOTES

NOTES